T0368090

A Guru In The Jungle

Aurora

A Guru In The Jungle

50 Lessons Learned on Relationships and Dating as a Woman on the Path

BALBOA.PRESS

A DIVISION OF HAY HOUSE

This book is a work of non-fiction. Unless otherwise noted, the author and the publisher make no explicit guarantees as to the accuracy of the information contained in this book and in some cases, names of people and places have been altered to protect their privacy.

Balboa Press books may be ordered through booksellers or by contacting:

Balboa Press
A Division of Hay House
1663 Liberty Drive
Bloomington, IN 47403
www.balboapress.com
844-682-1282

Because of the dynamic nature of the Internet, any web addresses or links contained in this book may have changed since publication and may no longer be valid. The views expressed in this work are solely those of the author and do not necessarily reflect the views of the publisher, and the publisher hereby disclaims any responsibility for them.

The author of this book does not dispense medical advice or prescribe the use of any technique as a form of treatment for physical, emotional, or medical problems without the advice of a physician, either directly or indirectly. The intent of the author is only to offer information of a general nature to help you in your quest for emotional and spiritual well-being. In the event you use any of the information in this book for yourself, which is your constitutional right, the author and the publisher assume no responsibility for your actions.

Any people depicted in stock imagery provided by Getty Images are models, and such images are being used for illustrative purposes only. Certain stock imagery © Getty Images.

Scripture quotations marked NIV are taken from the Holy Bible, New International Version®. NIV®. Copyright © 1973, 1978, 1984 by International Bible Society. Used by permission of Zondervan. All rights reserved. [Biblica]

Print information available on the last page.

ISBN: 979-8-7652-4692-4 (sc)
ISBN: 979-8-7652-4693-1 (e)

Library of Congress Control Number: 2023920882

Balboa Press rev. date: 10/31/2023

Dedication

I dedicate this book first and foremost to Spirit.
I'm listening now.

Thank You.

I also acknowledge with the utmost gratitude those
superstars on my "A-Team" who have tirelessly
and steadfastly supported me at my worst:

DWG, GS, SH, DR, CC, JB, AK, TW, DA

Thank You.

Furthermore, I am blessed to have several other "Angels"
in my life who have been there for me during this time:

KH, KS, JNC, DK, JP, my Counselors, my church's
Prayer Ministers, and everyone else who had lent
me their shoulder to cry on. I'll never forget it.

Thank You.

About the Author

Aurora is the author of four previous books and is the proud mother of two teenage children.

She teaches in the Youth Ministry at her church and works in Conferences & Events.

She has been interested in all things metaphysical most of her life but began studying and researching New Thought wisdom since the early 1990s. She is currently living in the Chicagoland suburbs with her kids, and their cat, Sami.

Table of Contents

Getting Back Out There Again – 231

The Road Ahead – 289

Preface

I really didn't want to write this book. However, Spirit kept bugging me about it, telling me to get it out of my system to heal and make sense of the incredibly painful experiences that have happened to me.

As with my other books, I write so that others may benefit from these lessons I've learned. Ideally, I hope that I could help at least one reader to never put themselves in a position that I did and avoid the tremendous pain that I suffered.

I needed to write this book just for me and my own healing, with no intention to get a reaction out of anyone or have to worry about what anyone is going to think of me. This is NOT a book to hurt anybody. This is a book to express MY hurt and to warn people NOT to do what I have done. I am not here to vilify anyone.

I wrote this in "stream-of-consciousness" style – exactly what was going through my head at the time – so that I can release all my pain and anger and replace it with forgiveness and some humor.

In my writing all these years, I've been telling people to "be your own Guru," but I was NOT my own Guru when it came to dating and relationships.

So, this book is a confession of sorts on how I completely and utterly gave my power away to other people … about holding a mirror to myself on how I have gotten to where I am now by not listening to my own guidance.

That is the danger of giving your power away in all things.

So, this book is my "swan song" about everything I've learned and to urge others that no matter what = Know thyself, have your boundaries, have your standards, and stick to them.

My highest prayer is that somebody will benefit from all of this that you're about to read and not make those same mistakes that I did. That's the very least I can offer. No one can guarantee anyone a happy ending except the one you make for your own – moving on from this is part of my happy ending.

I was my own Guru in the office, Guru being a mom, Guru with my food, and now I have to be the Guru of my dating and relationships and not get lost in my fears, insecurities, and past relationship trauma, which is exactly what happened.

I completely and utterly lost my rationale and turned over all my power to others in a recent situation, because dating and relationships have always been the one area I never felt in control of, since I have another person involved – it's not just me.

There were moments that I had emotion completely overwhelm me. It was as if it was all happening in front of me, and I couldn't do a thing to stop it.

This book is huge for me. I will admit to all of it.

Had I listened to myself, I wouldn't've gotten here.

I listened to other people who were well-meaning and sincerely tried to help me. However, I had one person who I thought had my back, but ultimately betrayed and backstabbed me, admitting that they hurt and sabotaged me on purpose.

So, this book is also about my healing and forgiveness for those who hurt me.

I very well could have simply titled this, "Why I Am Still Single."

I feel like those of us "on the path" of self-improvement and spirituality seem to also sometimes be very empathic, introspective, self-aware, and over-thinkers.

I know I am for sure.

I take a longer time than most to analyze and process my thoughts and emotions.

People like us have taken all sorts of workshops, read all the books, gone to counseling, done group therapy, taken classes, and are into all this "stuff," but because we tend to also be highly sensitive and emotional, when the "fit hits the shan," in romantic relationships, it seems like everything we've learned seems to go out the window.

Ultimately, this book is not only about the human tragedy of betrayal, heartbreak, abandonment, rejection, emotional abuse, and humiliation, but it's about digging deep inside yourself to find the Grace and Strength to learn the lessons, practice Forgiveness, and rise above it all.

In the years during my divorce, I got into the habit of saving messages – I had to for the case. Therefore, it became second nature to me.

Likewise, I got into the habit of taking pictures of my ingredients, preparation, and plating while cooking due to the two years I spent writing my last book on food.

I save messages that are important to me in some way – good, bad, funny – I have them all, and re-created a few here to the best of my ability to be able to tell the story.

The title referring to the "jungle," is an homage to the Guns 'N' Roses hit song, "Welcome to the Jungle," because I'm a child of the 80's – in particular, "hair band" or "arena rock" music.

Plus, the dating world IS quite the "jungle," isn't it?

The lyrics go:

> "Welcome to the jungle.
> It gets worse here every day.

You learn to live like an animal
in the jungle where we play."

I could not have written a better description of the dating scene today if I tried.

Thank you for being a part of my happy ending.

God bless you.

Enjoy!

Matthew 18:20 ~
"For where two or three
gather in my name,
there am I with them."

Luke 23:34 ~
And Jesus said,"Father, forgive them,
for they know not what they do."

"There is no perfect person that you find, it's who you make it work with." ~ Jay Shetty

"Your person is the one who can meet you where you're at and grow and heal with you." ~ Matthew Hussey

"When you are your best self, you can more clearly see who is for you and who is not." ~ Stephan Lebossiere

Getting Back Out There

Loki

I DIDN'T STEP INTO the dating world until almost a full year after my divorce was final on September 4, 2018. So, this was now around July-August 2019 timeframe. I joined Bumble, Twitter, and OK Cupid.

I'm calling this one "Loki," because my "best friend" at the time did me the favor of looking him up on the internet and discovered he had some kind of alias name on Twitter referring to himself as a "Chameleon," which was super-shady to us.

Although I found him online, he worked in the same place I did, and I remembered that we even had a meeting about a year or two ago on a project I was doing for my department at the time. So, I recognized him, and I was really excited about that, because I remember even then I was attracted to him right away.

I felt I could trust him, since he wasn't a "stranger," and he remembered me, too.

He was/is brilliant.

He's also handsome, tall (6'-6'2" at least), successful, accomplished, and has a second career saving lives, which I find incredibly admirable.

What was interesting, however, was that because he knew that he was my first attempt at a relationship since my divorce a year prior, he already thought of himself as my "rebound" man, but he didn't mind it.

Of course, I didn't like that idea and didn't appreciate going into it as such, so this experience was very brief.

Some things that turned me off quickly were that he didn't like concerts, had an "outie" belly button, and didn't put on his profile that he had a daughter.

He wasn't into being a dad, and I didn't like that at all.

I had him over for dinner once and he did something incredibly rude – he sat in my spot! He literally just helped himself and sat at the head of the table ... and that's MY spot. I am head of household here in my home. He didn't even ask me where he should sit. To me, it showed disrespect and lack of consideration.

The dealbreaker, however, was something I discovered after I told a co-worker that I saw him on one of my online dating apps. I didn't tell her that we were seeing each other, because we both wanted to keep that under wraps, but I wanted to see what she thought of him.

Turns out she said that he has a super-bad temper and that he has a history of raging against people in the organization so badly to the point where they complained to his boss because they were scared.

Plus, she said that he has another side business that is borderline stepping on what he does for our organization and his subordinates say that he's barely there and that they cover for him, bearing the brunt of the work, but he treats them like dirt and somehow gets away with it, because he's so high up on the ladder.

I believed what she was saying, because he already told me about his side work. Therefore, I knew she was telling the truth about everything else as well.

I felt sick.

So, I gently let the communication fade and we never spoke again.

No hard feelings, we just knew it was done.

I've never even seen him in person again, because the organization is so big, thank goodness!

LESSON: Always do an internet search on who you plan to date.

Adonis

So, THIS MAN TRULY was a creature of beauty. He was 30 and I was 47 at the time. He was tall (6'2" at least), athletic, and model-handsome, complete with brown hair, blue eyes, and a picture-perfect-toothpaste-commercial-dimpled smile.

He brought me back from the dead.

I felt like I had a "quickening," like in the movie "Interview With The Vampire."

He was my "How Stella Got Her Groove Back" man!

Except unlike the movie (fortunately!), I didn't catch feelings for him.

I am forever grateful to him, though, because this was now over a year and a half since Loki, because COVID hit, so I hadn't gone on any more dates.

It was late December 2020, and everything was mostly shut down, except I found this gem of a place that miraculously remained open throughout, because they brilliantly set up an "all-weather patio" outside, complete with live music. I named it my "Happy Place."

It was a godsend for a social person like me. I really struggled during the pandemic having to stay at home, but I was blessed to find some places with outdoor seating, thanks to a musician friend who told me where he was playing that had outdoor live music.

So, I went to my "Happy Place" one Saturday evening on a non-kid weekend, all bundled up in my large black winter coat, sweatpants, and gym shoes. I was barely even wearing much makeup. I just wanted to get out and have their delicious "Manzanilla Pizza" and listen to some live music, as I always did.

A group of young men took the empty seats near me, and Adonis chose the one next to me. I could see him out of the corner of my eye checking me out, so I glanced at him, and he smiled. He noticed my gym shoes and teased me about them.

Suddenly, we smelled something burning and noticed that one of the overhead heaters was a bit too close to the wooden plank directly behind Adonis' seat. He stood on the stool, reached up, and turned the heater off. I joked with him that he saved our lives, and the conversation took off from there.

He was "Cougar Bait," alright!

I wasn't too forward, but I couldn't help but respond to his flirtation. His friends wanted to go down the street, but he wanted to go to a place just across the way instead and invited me with.

I went.

I had my second post-divorce kiss that night, and wouldn't you know it … he suddenly couldn't get a hold of his friends who drove him, and he needed a ride home.

I was like, no way! He pleaded. I caved.

I drove him to his house, and we exchanged numbers. We had a very nice "goodbye," but I was a good girl and let him go inside alone.

That impressed him. He respected my boundaries and contacted me to take me out on a "real" date the next time I was available. He took me to a nice restaurant for dinner and we had a great conversation.

Turns out I was not the first older woman he's dated – that he actually prefers older women and has been "Cougar-hunting" for quite a while.

We saw each other only twice after that – once in January and once in May 2021, although he kept trying to meet me more, but my parenting schedule just wasn't lining up to when he wanted to see me.

Ultimately, my experience with him helped me realize that I really did want a "real" relationship after all.

LESSON: You never know when or where God will have you meet someone special – even wearing gym shoes!

Desmond

I'M CALLING THIS MAN "Desmond," from one of my favorite songs I enjoy singing with one of my "Karaoke Husbands." ("Karaoke Husband/Wife" is a term of endearment in the karaoke culture for a person who sings duets with you regularly and does NOT imply that you are a romantic couple, but only a "singing couple.")

I met Desmond on Bumble (this was now early February 2021), and he "checked all my boxes," except for one thing ... he was obese. He was upfront with me right away when we had our first "video date," and I appreciated that, but you know what – I didn't care. We hit it off well, and so he asked me out on a lunch date, and I agreed.

On the lunch date, I found his face even more attractive in person, despite his size. He explained that he was not always that size, and that he gained weight I think because of his divorce and showed me pictures of when he was thin.

He said he was working with a doctor and had a plan. I was very impressed, and I believed he would do it.

I really liked this guy. He did everything right. We kept messaging.

In conversation, I let him know about my church, in which we were still doing "Zoom Services" at the time and invited him to attend the upcoming Sunday's service.

He did!!!

I was so thrilled when I saw him log on, because he was Catholic, so I wasn't really expecting him to try it.

That was an A+ move in my book.

He was privately chatting with me during the service, which was making me laugh, so I had to turn off my video for a moment or two at certain points. He was SO charming!

He asked me out to dinner on the following Friday. We had a nice meal and conversation, then went somewhere else for a night cap.

We started talking about our divorces, but I made the huge mistake of unleashing my entire nightmare of a divorce process onto him!

We ended the night nicely, but the next day, he told me that he didn't think I was ready to date.

I was upset, but in hindsight, he was 100% correct. I was nowhere near ready.

He was handsome, tall (again, at least 6'), intelligent, accomplished, AND a good, proud father. I have no doubt he's achieved his weight loss goal and found his woman by now.

LESSON: Don't feel compelled to inundate a new partner with the tragic details of the demise of your previous relationship, and don't tell it too soon – if at all. Your history will naturally be shared when the time is right. And if you do choose to tell your story, the right partner will accept you with open arms and understand.

Van Hendrix

I AM USING THE pseudonym "Van Hendrix" for this one, because he is an extremely talented guitar player. His guitar collection is quite impressive, and he's been in a few bands.

We dated when I was in High School, and he lived in the same town. I was 17 and he was 19. I was so attracted to him – he was tall (6'1) and strong, with shoulder-length blonde hair, and gorgeous dimples. He wore glasses, so when he took them off, he joked that it was like he became Superman, which wasn't too far from the truth, if you catch my drift.

It ended up being just a "summer romance," because he broke up with me when he found out I kept a piece of information from him so that he wouldn't get angry. That is why I make it a point to never do that in a relationship since. I hadn't spoken to him until we found each other again on Facebook about the latter half of 2013, about 25 years later. He was still attractive to me, and me to him.

My marriage was falling apart, so he was a blessing for me. He tried to even help and offer advice, but my heart was fading out of it, and I was becoming more interested in this guy, feeling that God brought him into my life at this time for this very reason.

He told me that he regretted breaking up with me – that I was "the one who got away," that I was the "whole package" and that guys like my ex-husband really "pissed him off," because they have everything – a beautiful, intelligent, accomplished wife, great kids, a gorgeous house, a prosperous job – and are still miserable, and that he (my ex-husband) didn't deserve me.

He really brought my confidence back up with all these wonderful things he was saying to me! He made me feel heard and valued.

It wasn't meant to be, however, because he moved out of state shortly after.

Plus, he was a good man and didn't want to be a part of breaking up a family, so he kept his distance, and for that, I was grateful. I share that value with him to this day and never date men who are in the middle of a divorce.

We only kept in touch via Messenger and phone calls. He was also quite a talented writer and would write stories about us, which touched my heart.

Well, in early May 2018, we had a falling out on Facebook and I blocked him there and on my phone. After the 2021 Presidential inauguration ceremony, I created an entirely new Facebook account and he found me and "friended" me again. This was now somewhere in February 2021, and I had been divorced for years at this point, so he had no problem reconnecting with me.

Turns out he moved back to Illinois a year or so prior. He apologized for his part in our falling out. However, he let me know that he once again had to move back out of state in April for personal family reasons.

Regardless, we had a wonderful reunion in that short amount of time. We got to know each other all over again and had two wonderful dates until he left on Good Friday.

We still kept in touch and videochatted over Messenger.

He was always so kind and respectful to me. My Mom always liked him, which was a plus. We shared the same political views for the most part. He was very wise and knowledgeable about politics, so we had great conversations.

I especially loved it when he played guitar for me. I told him someday I wanted us to collaborate where he can play, and I can sing.

He was a blessing in my life, but just not meant to be. Over the years, our calls became fewer and far between.

I want a relationship where I have a man in my life – in person.

I wish him well always.

LESSON: Some relationships come into your life for a reason, but not meant to last.

Eros

Okay, now this one I started to catch feelings for, so writing this chapter is admittedly a tad rough for me …

He also found me on my new Facebook account in January 2021. I was excited that he found me, because we also went to high school together, like Van Hendrix, and he was also in "my crowd" – I recall we even went to a few parties together, although he was a year younger than me in class. I had fond memories of him being a funny, sweet guy, and so I was happy to have found another friend from "back in the day" to reminisce with.

At this point, however, we only "liked" or briefly commented on each other's posts, but nothing more, because it looked to me like he was married by the pictures, even though he had nothing on his status, and so I wasn't going to touch that with a 10-foot pole.

After Van Hendrix left in April, I posted something a week later like, "Lord help me, I'm going back on the sites! Wish me luck!!" and he messaged me this:

Which ones?
Imma swipe right!

I don't date married men!
Nice try!

> I get that!
> Separated for a few years but
> I know what cha mean!

So, he said "a few years," from which I assumed that meant they had filed for divorce and were almost done now, because the average time it takes to divorce is two years, especially with kids. That's how long mine took.

Therefore, I thought in this case, it was safe to let this happen, because he was almost done.

I was naïve and thought he was "safe," so I invited him out to meet me and my "best friend" at the time at my "Happy Place."

Total sparks.

We had an amazing time and immediately he started messaging me how interested he was, and things sped up from there.

I was totally taken with him. We had the same political views (which was a priority to me at the time), same love of our children and parenting them, he was also a corporate professional, had an impressive LinkedIn profile, handsome as heck, funny as hell, sober, and spiritual.

On top of it, he was a Scorpio, like my ex-boyfriend when I was in my 20's, so we had insane chemistry, for what that's worth …

I felt like this was it! I did the work, I'm ready, and this is my reward.

We met up a few times, but never on an actual "date" out anywhere, so that should have been my first red flag.

Second red flag is that the next couple of times we were set to meet up, he flaked and cancelled, making excuses.

Final red flag for me was as I got to figure out his schedule, I discovered that he had a rather "fluid" parenting schedule with his kids' mom – he went to the marital home regularly, saw his kids every day (meaning he saw HER every day), worked with her, was connected with her on social media where she'd always "like" and/ or comment on his posts …

The nail in the coffin, however, was that I did some digging on his county website and discovered … they hadn't ever actually FILED for divorce! – they were only meeting with a mediator, who also happened to be a mutual friend.

All of this was way too much for me, and I was utterly heartbroken.

Fortunately, a month or so prior, I saw an ad on Facebook to start a summer sand volleyball league and became captain of a team I pulled together with my "best friend" at the time, so I had something else to focus on.

I also chose to do a dry month and called it "Attune June" and focus on myself and healing from this situation.

I vowed NEVER to date anyone who is only "separated" EVER again.

Besides, God put someone else in my life around this point, so I made the decision to let Eros go and to pay more attention to this other guy – "Him."

LESSON: Only date someone emotionally available.

The Ordeal

Intuition

"You're so pretty!" she said, laughing.

He was laughing, too — my date.

They both sat there laughing at me.

This was our first date, late July 2021, after my "best friend" introduced us a few months prior. She was there because she was going through something serious in her life and we were both "best friends" with her.

Earlier that evening, however, when she said she was bored and wanted to go out, I simply told her I had plans.

But then, she called "Him" — and "He" picked her up … with no hesitation … without checking in with me first, since he and I already made plans.

I guess neither one of us had the heart to tell her that this was supposed to be our first date.

I replied to her, "So, you're calling me stupid?"

"Oh, no! It's just a joke! You've never heard of that before?" she asked.

No, I haven't, but it didn't sound good. So, later I looked up the phrase "You're so pretty" in the Urban Dictionary and this is what it says:

"Response to a completely inarticulate comment made by someone who should focus mostly on looking attractive to become successful. Verbal communication by this person is likely to cause embarrassment to this person and to those around her."

She said this to me because I was figuring out what to order on the menu.

That single decision to let her come with us on our first date colored our relationship from then on out.

It was supposed to be a selfless act … putting her well-being above our budding romance.

Finding love is just a crap shoot, anyway, right???

Who's to say if it was going to even work out or not?

I mean, it was only our first date …

Unfortunately, there will be several more intensely painful lessons to come for me, but this was one that could have possibly saved me all the rest, had I been more aware and handled it right then.

Seeing them both laughing at me together, I should have ended things with him right then and there.

Something didn't sit well with me about that moment.

Right then, I should have stopped and figured out the extent of their relationship and my feelings for him, and how that was all going to work before going one step further ...

I should have done some honest self-evaluation to see if I was going to be comfortable with him having that level of emotional intimacy with her ... and gauge that with the emotional intimacy that him and I were developing in our new relationship together on a romantic level.

I didn't do any of that important analysis.

I went too fast with him.

I got too carried away with my feelings and lost my rationale.

I should have put boundaries on my friendship with her and my romantic relationship with him right then.

We BOTH should have (he and I).

There were a couple of good things I do remember about that night ...

One was that when I was sitting at the table waiting for him to arrive, he texted me that he was picking her up, so I was talking with a girlfriend on the phone to pass the time.

I was facing the door of the restaurant and ... he walked in!

I was in shock because he said he was picking her up. I told my friend, "OMG, he's here! I gotta go!"

He walked right up to me, and I said, "What happened? I thought you were picking her up!"

He goes, "I am, but I was just about here already and there's something more important that I had to do first …"

And then he kissed me.

I just about melted.

Right then and there, I should have had the sense to suggest that he let her find another friend to hang out with that night and let us have our first date alone …

But I didn't think. I was too scared to express my feelings.

I didn't want to be "the bad guy," and be selfish in her time of need … even though she knew full well we were supposed to be on a date.

So, the other good thing he did was when we were ordering our appetizers, she said she wanted a certain one and he looked straight at her and said …

"This isn't about you."

I had the feeling he was also feeling slighted that this night was supposed to be ours and she shouldn't've been there.

Had I listened to my feelings, how different things could have been …

This was the very night that started the issue.

LESSONS:

* Trust your intuition. If something doesn't "feel" right, even if you can't adequately explain it in words at the moment, do not ignore this feeling. Sit with this feeling and keep exploring it until the right words come.

* There needs to be boundaries between friendships and romantic relationships.

Girl Code

IT WAS NOW A full three months since she introduced us, and by then we both had established our strong interest in each other.

Therefore, I naively assumed that if they had any history, she would have told me by now, since I considered her my "best friend" at the time, and that's just "Girl Code."

We had been hanging out closely for almost two years at this point, but oddly, I didn't even know this guy existed, before she texted me sometime in April saying, "My friend likes you and wants to meet you."

I came to find she had been telling HIM about ME for quite a while.

I mean, maybe she had mentioned him to me in passing, but she always mentioned her vast array of male friends/ex-lovers, including her ex-husband, in passing, so I just didn't pay attention.

In hindsight, I feel it's pretty shady that I didn't even know about this guy whatsoever in almost two entire years of us hanging out and even going on a 5-day vacation out of the country with her – nothing about him whatsoever.

But ... something she said that night "hit" me a certain way, and so I finally asked the question ...

"Hey, wait, did you and he ever …?"

"Of course!" she happily exclaimed.

Wow.

Just. Wow.

It was a punch to the gut learning that I was kept in the dark all these months.

Now, my mind was spinning with more questions …

How much longer would this information have been kept from me had I not asked the question?

Are they "friends with benefits?" … Is that why they are so close??

Is that why I never heard about this guy??

Was she keeping him under wraps for herself and only introduced us because HE bugged her to do so???

In almost TWO whole years since we reconnected and were hanging out socially – even going on vacation out of the country together! – I've never met him at all … but NOW all of a sudden, I come to find that they're "best friends," and her kids call him "uncle," and her parents call him their "third son." WTH??

How was it possible that she didn't tell me ANY of that before introducing me to this guy? She just said, "my friend." All that is a HECK of a lot more than "just a friend." She didn't tell the truth.

She said it was a "one-time thing," but how can I believe that now?

In fact, how could I believe her about ANYTHING anymore?

Her response set the stage for several months ahead of me trying to figure out the truth about the relationship between them via discussions, to which she vacillated between remarks such as "Mmmmm, he'd look SO good if he got his teeth fixed!" and "Mmmm, Southside Irish!" (which made literally NO sense, since he was raised in the suburbs) to "Ew, I could never date him." and "He doesn't know how to treat women."

Years of trust broken.

If she found him attractive, then she should have just admitted it, instead of gaslighting me like she did.

One thing I cannot stand is a liar.

The other thing I can't stand is when people keep me in the dark.

Secrets and lies just aren't my thing.

One day, she finally decided to answer me about why she didn't tell me upfront and said ...

"None of my other friends would have cared. I didn't think anything of it. We've never talked about it since until YOU keep bringing it up. It's no big deal."

She said that she told her ex-husband what happened before they married, and that he didn't care.

But, she didn't tell ME upfront before introducing us ... I had to ASK.

The purpose of "Girl Code" is women protecting women. Especially "Do right by people you call close girlfriends."

Simple things like:

- making sure a woman is inside the house before driving away

- rescuing any woman being harassed by a man in public

- checking in on a woman who is crying or looks scared

- defending a woman in her absence

- never abandoning a drunk woman

- never keeping secrets FROM her that could affect her safety or wellbeing

- keeping HER secrets FOR her that could affect her safety or wellbeing

Women are supposed to lift each other up. But these days, some women will do anything to boost their own ego and play victim to get male attention.

It's sad.

Very little integrity left.

Also, according to my standards and boundaries, when you have sex with someone, you are ex-lovers.

I just didn't appreciate the fact that they are pretending they are "just friends."

To me, saying they were "just friends" meant they ALWAYS were ONLY "friends" and nothing more.

I feel it's deceptive.

I personally am not "just friends" with anyone I have been intimately involved with.

I don't even have them as "friends" on social media.

That's my personal boundary and standard.

Even if many folks disagree, I'm okay with that.

It keeps things clear, protects my heart, and my future partner's heart.

LESSONS:

* When someone sets you up with somebody of the opposite sex that they claim is "a friend," make sure you find out the extent of their history first, and if you're comfortable with that, before you consider pursuing that relationship.

* A person's ethics and morals regarding intimacy are a personal choice, so it's important to be on the same page as

your partner in that regard, keeping in mind that no one is "better" or "worse" for how they choose to conduct themselves, because we are all God's children.

However, it is important to remember that YOU are also God's child and deserve to have what it is you're looking for as well and don't need to abide by what anyone else thinks is right.

Respect yourself; honor your boundaries.

* Don't let anyone minimize your feelings. Do not dismiss your feelings or let anyone talk you out of them. Your feelings sometimes know more than your brain does — which is especially true in the realm of romantic relationships because certain emotions can be powerful enough to release a myriad of chemicals in our brain that often affect our logical thinking.

The Breakup

So, I "GOT OVER" the idea of them two together and chose to pursue a relationship with him. We started dating. He was so thoughtful and creative with our dates! He really impressed me.

We became closer and closer to the point we made the decision to become "Facebook Official" on Saturday, September 18, 2021.

Which I later come to find that's something called "First Love Day" …

Interesting coincidence …

Yet, he preferred the date of September 15 for us to mark as our starting date, because he said that's when we first walked into our game holding hands that Wednesday night.

I didn't even realize that until he said it.

I was SO incredibly touched!

He always remembered the little things about me like that.

About us.

He's got an incredible memory – I could count on HIS memory better than mine, sometimes.

We still had serious differences, though, and I was scared.

I was very much on guard – I didn't trust myself and didn't trust him yet, although I really wanted to.

One weekend, we were deciding what to do on a Saturday night, and we came up with three options.

One of the options was going to a local concert and meeting his friends.

I love live music, so I chose that one.

I made the mistake of telling her ...

She goes, "Oh, he only wants to show you off to his friends."

That really got to me.

"Show me off to his friends?" Like, I was some kind of notch in his bedpost?? Like, I didn't mean anything to him at all? Just his current bimbo, is that it?

Well, we went to the concert, and I noticed the entire night he was looking around waiting for his friends, making comments about where they are and such. He was really getting anxious.

... and I was getting more and more upset.

I felt like he didn't even care about spending time with me. He didn't seem to be enjoying the concert at all, just looking around for his friends.

Finally, one couple in his friend group came by us and it was nice to meet them, they were great. Turned out the lady's name was the same as mine, so we were joking about that.

What seemed like forever, eventually his other friends came that he especially wanted to see, and he was ecstatic. I was happy for him, and they all seemed like nice people, but I felt significantly out of place.

My insecurities started creeping in.

After the concert was over, we had the option to leave or walk to the bar across the street. I was really tired, and we hadn't had dinner, and I wanted to go home, but I knew he was waiting all evening to see his friends whom he hadn't seen in a long time …

… so AGAIN, I didn't speak up for myself.

… AGAIN, I didn't want to "be the bad guy," and so, I agreed to go to the bar.

On the way walking there, one of his closest friends turned to me and said, "So, you're a 'tree-hugger,' huh?" He was smiling, so I guess it was meant to be a joke of some kind, but I owned it and I go, "Yeah, I guess!"

But, in the back of my mind, it made me feel like he was "calling me out," letting me know that I didn't fit in with their group, and that my time was limited.

Of course, that was all in my head, but I was already irritated by what she said earlier in the day and her words echoed in my head the entire time.

He was certainly happier now that they were there. What did he need ME there for? He'd been waiting for THEM all night and now they were there, and he was having a great time.

So, we all sat at a table outside talking and I was feeling more and more uncomfortable, and by then, I've had a bit more to drink than I should have, and we still didn't eat anything, so I had to go to the bathroom.

I went inside, found it, but instead of going back to the table afterward, I went to the inside bar and ordered a beer for myself to have, feeling pretty low. Then, a young girl there with her boyfriend started up a conversation with me about relationships.

I love talking to people and can talk to anyone for hours, regardless of the situation. Well, in this particular situation, I completely lost track of time and suddenly he came inside, spotted me, and waved his finger angrily at me to come by him, but I didn't like that attitude, so I held up one finger to say "Hold on a sec."

Apparently, that was the wrong answer …

He left.

He literally started walking home.

He left me there alone …

… having had a bit too much to drink

… at a strange bar I've never been before

… to figure out how to get home by myself

… in front of all his friends I just met.

He didn't care if I lived or died …

… got raped

… got beaten

… got robbed

… or got home at all.

No guy had EVER done that to me before in my ENTIRE life!

Needless to say, I ended the relationship the next day.

He literally abandoned me!

It was an absolute dealbreaker.

But what did I do …??? … My brain started over-thinking.

… I started back-tracking and trying to figure out what went wrong.

I traced it back to her text earlier that day, "Oh, he's only showing you off to his friends."

How nice it would have been if she instead had said, "Hey, tonight is important to him – he's having you meet his friends – that's a big step! Congratulations! Have a great time!"

How nice it would have been to have had that kind of encouragement and support for us in our new relationship!

I had no idea what it meant. I only discovered over a YEAR later in my research on relationships that it was probably an important step for him in our relationship to set up that meeting.

I hadn't been at the very beginning of a relationship in over 2 decades!

I totally forgot the steps of integration into each others' lives … that meeting each other's "people" was a huge thing …

On the other hand, I should NOT have let her words spiral in my brain like it did.

… but this experience sure taught me a big lesson.

Unbelievably, our relationship didn't end with this incident, although this was definitely the first "beginning of the end".

However, unfortunately, things were never quite the same between us after that incident.

LESSONS:

* First instincts are often correct. Had I never spoken to this man again, I could have saved myself so much future pain, grief, and a friendship.

* If in doubt about something you heard about your partner, ask THEM. Do NOT make assumptions.

I should have clarified what the purpose of the date really was. I should have had more confidence in myself, that perhaps he really wanted to be with me and that he felt I was important enough to be introduced to his friends, instead of the other way around that I had it in my head.

Casual

IN TRYING TO COPE with all that's happened in the writing of this book, I did a lot of self-reflection on what my part was in getting myself into this nightmare, and I can probably pinpoint it to one bad decision (among many!) ... my proposing that we have a "casual" relationship.

This was entirely my own stupid decision, which I quickly regretted about a month in, but something told me to just wait it out.

What happened was after our breakup, I took a few days to cool off and tried to look at the entirety of him and our time together, instead of just the incident that happened, and I realized that he had a lot of good qualities, and that he was going to be in my life as long as I was still friends with her, and there was no way I wanted to be "just friends" with him.

Absolutely no way.

So, I thought, well, maybe this was my opportunity to try this "casual" thing everyone else is doing and speaks so highly of. Maybe we can enjoy each other's company when able, without the commitment of being tied down.

What an utter fool I was!

I NEVER normally do that, because I know myself better that I would get too attached, and that I just don't believe in the concept, because I want a committed, exclusive relationship.

Although I never really wanted to do this, I just figured I'd give it a try and see if he'd be interested, and so a mere two weeks after the breakup, I contacted him and invited him to talk at what I call "my local happy place."

It turned out to be one of the best evenings we had together.

We talked about what happened with the breakup, because I thought that when he walked away and left me there that HE was the one breaking up with ME, but to my utter shock, he goes …

"I wasn't even mad the next day!"

Well, dang. Egg on my face!

But, gosh, that was a pretty brutal move, so I was correct in breaking it off with him, anyways.

Or, was I? …

Something really crazy happened when I tried to go onto Facebook that next day after he left me at the bar to change my relationship status … the entire Facebook app was down!!!

And, not just for a few minutes … it was down for quite a while! Hours.

I almost took that as a sign that God was wanting me to think about this … that maybe I should talk to him first before I just arbitrarily changed my relationship status.

Normally, I always DO pay attention to "signs" like that because I believe God guides me in my time of need.

But … nope, I ignored that chance to stop and think.

I was too emotional.

During this evening's "meetup," however, we had another great conversation where I learned more about him, and in fact, I can pinpoint that very night as one of the moments my feelings for him went to a higher level.

After we got home, we had a beautiful exchange where he let me know that he got home and I told him I felt the night was amazing, like it somehow felt like a first date, and that we had great conversation and that he looked great.

His reply was that it was easy to look great when he was with me, that I brought it out of him, and agreed it was a great night.

I'm home.

Good baby. I'm glad!

It was amazing tonight, the whole thing.

It felt like a first date for some reason, LOL!

We had a great conversation and you looked great.

I love your look. Your facial hair and what you were wearing. It really suits you, babe!

Sleep well!

Thank you honey. But it's easy to look great when I'm with you.
You bring it out of me and yes. It was a great night.

Yet, I ignored that feeling, and instead, foolishly proposed my "let's do casual" idea, and that was the agreement we had since October 20, 2021.

What an idiot I was!

Over the next several months, we found ourselves in what I now know is the term "Situationship." We kept spending time together, kept making plans – Halloween, Christmas Eve, and New Year's – which all got ruined because of the COVID-19 virus, but we were able to spend Christmas Eve and New Year's Eve together via Zoom.

He made us Christmas Eve dinner that I went to pick up by his door and I gave him a present. I brought the food back home and we ate together over videochat. (We did it this way, because I thought I had COVID, but over a week later, the test came back negative.)

I mentioned what he'd done to a friend afterward and he said, "Oh, the Wigilia!" ... so, of course, I looked it up on the Internet ... and it says on Wikipedia:

> Wigilia (Polish pronunciation: [vʲiˈɡʲilja]) is the traditional Christmas Eve vigil supper in Poland, held on December 24. The term is often applied to the whole of Christmas Eve, extending further to Pasterka—midnight Mass, held in Roman Catholic churches all over Poland and in Polish communities worldwide at or before midnight. The custom is sometimes referred to as "wieczerza" or "wieczerza wigilijna", in Old Polish meaning evening repast, linked to the late church service, Vespers from the Latin.

This, to me, was awesome, because I am over half Polish, and I'm sure he didn't even realize he'd done this. He's not one ounce of Polish blood that I'm aware of, but it warmed my heart, because I felt it was just another sign that I should have paid attention to.

A week later we watched the ball drop together on New Year's Eve over videochat to welcome in 2022.

Also in December, we even made plans for a big trip together in early February, in which we had SO much fun planning! We were both really excited about it, and I felt we grew even closer.

I was faithful and loyal to him, even though we weren't an "official" couple.

I never lied to him.

I always tried to lift his spirits when he was down.

I did my very best to support him in whatever it was he needed to do – right from the start.

Right up until the end – in his new job, which I knew meant the end of us.

The more I learned about him during our hours and hours of conversation – his character, his history, his goals – the more I was impressed by him, and the more my feelings grew.

He really surprised me.

I was hooked.

That's why I always told him he was amazing.

He simply fascinated me.

Unfortunately, little did I know in the last half of our relationship, as my feelings for him were growing, his feelings for me were fading.

We never had that discussion about what we felt for each other, so we never knew.

I suppose part of that was because I did not ask the question.

... because we agreed we were just "casual."

He was very clear with me around this time that he was in a bad place. It just wasn't the right time, and I knew it.

And I did not clarify what it was that I wanted because I didn't even really know within myself at the time ...

And that is the important part about being alone awhile and really getting to know yourself and what you need in a partner, if any.

Perhaps if I told him that she said that he only wanted to "show me off" to his friends at the concert that night, I could have asked him what meeting his friends really meant to him instead of letting it fester inside me and walking away from him, causing him to be upset and walk away from me.

Perhaps if I told him the next day how devastating it was to me when he left me there – when he said he wasn't even mad anymore – we would have apologized, understood each other better, and not broken up at that time.

Perhaps if I told him how I was really feeling and found out if he was feeling the same way, he would have tried a little harder to find a local job and stay.

So many things I should have told him.

LESSONS:

* Don't ever agree to a "casual" relationship with someone you have feelings for, thinking that will somehow make the issue of conflict obsolete with there being "no obligation." I promise you, you will get hurt, because you are being dishonest with yourself and with your partner.

In these "casual situationships," there are no boundaries, no clarity, and no security; thus, these unclear expectations lead to conflict.

* If you are blessed to have someone in your life you are happy being coupled with, let them know how you feel about them.

* If the feelings are mutual, lock it down, and then proceed do what it takes to make it work, riding the natural challenges that will cross your path by working through them, because you feel being with that person is worth it.

Third-Party Interference

"He says you're 'too happy and peppy' and that you 'need to tone it down a bit.'"

This she declared – unprovoked – out of the blue in front of a mutual friend as a concert we were attending was about to start in early January.

I was humiliated, surprised, and very hurt. I mean, I've never had a guy tell me I'm "too happy" before.

Interestingly, she's done this to me several times before by telling me things like "He thinks ..." and "He told me ..." and, "That's not what HE said ...!" and it was upsetting to me each time.

One day, I told her I didn't like that, that they should not be talking about me behind my back like that.

Her response was, "We never talk about you, we talk about our own $#!+!"

Okay ...

Well, thank goodness I had a witness. Our mutual friend later told me she was upset for me, because that happened to her as well – someone interfering in her relationship – and that ended badly also, so she could relate to me and my situation.

46

My friend said she thought to herself, "What is *she* doing being in the middle like that? Who is *she* to tell that to my friend?" but she knew I was "best friends" with her at the time, so she didn't butt in. I didn't find out her feelings about what she'd witnessed until months later.

I wish she'd HAD butt in. Maybe I would have woken up sooner and somehow taken action to salvage both relationships.

Because it happened again, a few weeks later …

We were at a restaurant with a different mutual friend and the friend turned to me in front of her and asked me how things were going with him.

It was going very well at the time, and I proceeded to tell the mutual friend all about the upcoming trip we'd had planned coming up the following week, when suddenly "She" blurts out, "He's got a special nickname for me, you know … he calls me 'Babe'!"

Our mutual friend's eyes got very wide, and she turned to her and goes, "He calls you BABE???" with a disgusted look on her face …

Again, I was humiliated.

Mortified, more like it, this time.

That comment totally angered me and embarrassed me in front of our mutual friend.

... like, I'm involved with and going on vacation the following week with a man who calls another woman "Babe."

... and then she right away tried to backpedal and switched it to "Sweetheart."

"Oh, wait," she said, "It's not 'Babe,' it's 'Sweetheart.'"

Okay ...

Cute side note here ... my ex-husband DID have a "special nickname" for her = "Sprite." He said that's what she reminded him of, probably because she was so thin and had a bright personality. It suited her well.

Then, she drops a bomb on both of us about something serious from his past that we had NO business knowing!

The mutual friend and I were in total shock that she would tell us something SO personal about him for literally NO reason.

I felt so bad for him! But, again, I never told him.

I knew he would be very angry at her for telling us that, and I didn't want to start trouble between them.

That's just not who I am.

Afterward, she and I had another "discussion" about her comments she just made in front of our mutual friend ... which didn't go well, as you can imagine.

Given all these statements she'd been saying to me both in private and in front of our mutual friends … and telling me things about him I had NO business knowing just yet …

My relationship with him never had a chance to progress naturally.

… and as I said, I never told him ANY of this.

I was in an impossible position.

Had I told him the things she'd been saying to me all along, I would have looked petty.

He wouldn't have believed me.

They were too close.

It would have just backfired on me.

Relationships can be challenging enough in today's world as it is, especially at our age, so we only had a 50/50 chance, regardless …

… and then to consider each of our own past relationship trauma and individual personal issues …

… and then throw an outside influence in – especially one who was now sabotaging us …

… we had NO chance.

She ended up saying she regretted introducing us. She says, "it never should have happened." That was the one thing I DID tell him that she said – and he told me that she told him that, too.

I said, "I don't regret it at all, though."

And he said, "Neither do I."

So, at least I know at some point, he and I were on the same page, and, of course, I happen to believe that God doesn't make mistakes.

What I DO regret is positioning her as the middleperson early on. That was a huge mistake on my part, and from all these comments (and many more!) that she's said to me, it sounded like he did the same thing, as in this text:

> I told him several times to just leave me out of it.

She "told him several times" to leave her out of it, huh?

We BOTH drove her crazy, poor thing!

I don't know why he did it, but strictly speaking for myself, I did this because I was scared. This was the first real relationship I've had since my divorce. I had NO idea what I was doing. I went to her for advice on everything about him because she's known him even longer than she knew me, which was decades.

I trusted her.

But, of course, I don't entirely blame her because that's not fair. I should have known better and kept her out of it and communicated to him myself, like a grown woman, not a scared little girl.

I should have trusted myself.

I only wish I would have met him separate from her, but it's too late now.

I take full responsibility for my part in this, but there were 3 parts = my part, his part, and her part.

He and I both went to her, telling her things about the other and asking for advice. At least I know I did.

She said right there in the text that he was doing the same.

That poisoned our relationship instead of enhancing it.

I should not have gone to her about him at all.

I should have talked to HIM directly about us.

He should not have gone to her about me.

We should have gone to each other.

And, if we wanted advice, then we should have gotten it from a far-removed person – someone that didn't know any of us – that would have been more fair.

I shared what was going on with a far-removed friend who gave me solid advice, but I was ignorant at the time, and I didn't listen.

She should not have engaged — should not have said anything to either one of us.

She was too close to us both.

It was doomed from the start by her opening her mouth like that.

I wonder what would have been like if I met him on my own without her interference.

It really is a tragedy, but it's a lesson learned.

I would never ever do that again, and I would not advise it to any one of you out there.

If you find yourself in a situation like this, please note this — I hope you're learning something from this book.

If you are the one in the middle of two people that you introduced — not in the romantic relationship ...

Please leave them alone!

Don't offer advice or information that neither one of them should know!

Let their relationship develop on their own!

LESSONS:

* Never allow a third party to interfere with your romantic relationship — even if they are well-meaning, even if they are family, even if they know you both well. They should NEVER

be given that kind of power over you two. Relationships are challenging enough to maintain without adding an outside influence into the mix when they have no purpose there. A relationship is between two people.

* Nobody has the authority to speak on behalf of anyone else, no matter how long they've known each other. So, if somebody tries to speak on behalf of your partner, discuss it directly with your partner as soon as possible.

* Never be afraid to talk to your partner about issues involving third-party interference – it is important to give them a chance to see how they react – to find out if you are on the same page regarding the value of your relationship.

This is especially important if this interference is happening in a new relationship – never assume what your partner will do or say about it, because you just don't know them well enough yet. It is best to communicate what is on your mind and in your heart as soon as you are able, rather than living with the regret of what they will never know.

The Matchmaker

IT'S FUNNY HOW SOMETIMES things happen so fast that we often don't have time to process it quickly enough to respond appropriately.

It's always been a challenge for me, and that's why I write. I'm not quick with in-person responses, because I analyze too much.

We were at her close relative's wake at her parents' house, and he was there along with a few members of her extended family. She and I were in the kitchen talking with her aunt, and he was in the living room.

Her aunt asked about him – who he was and why he was there, and she explained. Then, out of the blue she tells her aunt, "Aurora and he used to date."

I was floored. I had NO idea why in the world she thought that was a good idea to bring that up in that moment. I felt it was totally inappropriate.

Now, I was in an impossible situation – once again!

First of all, yes, we "used to" be an official couple, but secondly (and, most importantly) – we were STILL "involved."

We weren't all over each other, because she made it crystal clear to both of us that she wasn't a fan of our relationship – she told us both that she regretted introducing us.

Plus, we agreed not to be an official couple at this time, since he was starting a new job and leaving the state in a matter of days. It wasn't the time or place for us to "present" like that.

So, what was she trying to say ... that she didn't know that we were still involved? Of course, she did! She's been there every step of the way! In fact, I just shared with her a personal breakthrough he and I had in our relationship the other day! What was she trying to pull here, putting me on the spot like this??

Coincidentally, her aunt happened to be into New Age material, such as I was, and in particular, zodiac signs. So, she proceeds to walk into the living room and analyze all our signs. She mistook me for an air sign, which was quite good, because although I am a water sign, I have heavy air in my chart – Libra rising and a Gemini moon – which explains why my most prominent relationships were with air and fire signs. Even the one in my 20's I mention elsewhere in this book, although he was a Scorpio, his birthday was on November 21st, so he was more on the cusp of Sagittarius, which is a fire sign.

Then, her aunt goes up to him and compliments him on his eyes, and then turns to her and announces "Oh, you and he are (and she names their water and fire signs) so that's compatible! You two would be quite a couple if you guys ever wanted to give it a go!"

I was INCENSED.

This lady says this RIGHT in front me.

After she JUST told her that we "used to date."

All three of us were just standing there looking at each other in complete silence.

The joke was that she was totally wrong, based strictly on the zodiac signs she named, anyway. Water and Fire generally do NOT go together – they are not compatible. Water and Water or Water and Earth go together. Fire goes with Air.

He and I got along well because, yes, I have a lot of Air in my chart, and he was Fire. I never did his chart, however, so I have no idea what his rising sign or moon sign is, but it could explain some things.

Later, after the wake was over, and her aunt was gone, she tells me, "Did you see him and I looking at each other like what the heck?"

Ummm, no, I didn't. All this time, I didn't want to EVER think about them two together!

Why was she rubbing her aunt's comment in my face like that? It hurt me enough that it even happened – because she had to bring up to her that he and I "used to date."

Why didn't I just speak up that we WERE still involved when she told her aunt that?

Why didn't I let her aunt know?

Because it wasn't the time or place, I assessed.

I had tact.

Never again will I hold my tongue when there's an opportunity for the truth to be misrepresented like that.

LESSON: Speak up!!! The truth needs to be told, always. Nothing good ever comes from withholding relevant information. Secrets and lies only make things worse. Even the Bible says that "the Father sees all things in secret" – the truth always comes out in the end.

Communication

I RECALL WHEN THINGS were getting serious, he was on my couch talking and he said, "We'll be alright as long as we communicate."

Well, I tried my best, but I realize there is such a thing as "talking," "texting," and "writing," but you also need to "listen to understand."

We talked a lot. I absolutely loved our conversations. Unfortunately, we didn't tell each other the things we really needed each other to know.

We didn't ask the right questions, either.

Plus, our form of communication was off. Now that I've done the research, I know better what to do in this regard.

You see, I'm a writer (duh!). He was not. He hated it when I texted and wrote to him too much. It was entirely the wrong approach with him.

This guy was the first guy I dated in decades who didn't have a desk job. The last guy who didn't have a desk job I dated was in my early 20's – he was a mechanic, my Scorpio, and we were together for 6 years, living together for 4. The ending of that relationship cut me deeply, and it was just a year or so later that I met my ex-husband.

My ex-husband and I both had desk jobs, engaged only 6 months in, then married for 17 years, and for all these years we would write each other letters all day long. In fact, we "met and fell in love" online (via Yahoo Personals) writing each other very lengthy letters for days (maybe for a couple weeks?) before we met in person.

So, that was my main form of communication with my ex. We'd literally have entire conversations (and arguments) in lengthy letters to each other in-between working – and resolve everything by 4:30 p.m., Monday-Friday. No joke.

With this guy, he actually wanted to TALK to me (what???) – and, not on the phone – only on video call. I think it was because he liked seeing me.

I recall over my kids' winter break in December 2021, he video called me out of the blue, simply because he said he missed seeing my face.

Again – I was SO deeply touched!!

I took them to an arcade, and I stepped just outside the front door to chat with him, so I could see him better and converse with him in private.

It was brilliant. In-person/in "real life" communication truly is the best communication medium possible.

… EXCEPT if you're a person like me who has a lot to say and needs to write her ideas down on the screen to organize them in the best way possible to make sure I've said everything I wanted to say in the best way possible. (I'm being facetious, but only partly …)

For me, writing is the only way to make sure I'm not interrupted, side-tracked, or lose my train of thought.

Plus, if anyone tries to say, "she said this …" and it's not true, I can show them the message as proof. It's all right there in black-and-white.

Yet, I've learned the hard way, too, that someone can literally look at the same message and see something completely different, which is mind-boggling to me, but possible.

That happened in the case of me and her. In the instance of comparing apples and oranges, apples can have a productive conversation with other apples. Oranges can have a productive conversation with other oranges. Some people I thought were apples turned out to be oranges. Some people I assumed were oranges turned out to be apples and surprised me.

In a relationship, compatibility is key, no matter how big your differences may be to the person looking in. But, if you can't have a productive conversation with someone, it's never going to work.

Furthermore, it's important to determine if the person you're trying to communicate with is even operating with the same cognitive abilities or awareness as you.

I learned that it's important I become mindful of that when I start to get angry about what people have said and done and instead extend grace, patience, understanding, compassion, and most of all, forgiveness, because there's a chance that we're not comparing apples to apples here.

He told me not to message him so much – that he couldn't read it while he was working, so I stopped. In fact, after he got a new job early April, I stopped too much. I went completely cold – against my better judgment, but by "advice from a friend".

So much so, that I got the cutest message from him on Facebook Messenger the morning of April 21, 2022 (ironically, my ex-anniversary):

> U remember me lol

My heart absolutely melted! God, what I WANTED to reply to him was that he'd never left my thoughts and that I missed him terribly! But, I think I probably responded something that sounded pretty indifferent, just to try and remain cool and not needy.

As painful as it was for me, I held off and didn't bother him with my usual numerous texts and essays. It killed me not to message him every day, I missed him so much, but I refrained, because I didn't know his schedule and I didn't want to bug him on his new job.

I did something different – I waited for HIM to reach out in order to respect his time – despite the fact that I missed him terribly, and aside from the fact that he never said goodbye to me before he left, which he knew was the ONE thing I wanted.

I was damned if I did, and damned if I didn't, because I just didn't know how to properly communicate with him at the time.

We had some big plans early February – so big, that I felt the fate of our entire relationship was dependent upon these plans going through. Our vacation. We'd have uninterrupted alone time where we could really talk – in person – about all this stuff going through my head for quite a while that I wanted to finally resolve.

Well, our plans didn't work out, so instead, I wrote him a lengthy letter, disclosing all my fears, all my personal baggage, all my questions ... and it was a disaster. It all came out the wrong way, and he didn't reply to me.

I made the mistake of telling her I wrote him this letter and she asked me if he replied yet after a day or so, but he had not.

I told her to please drop it, because in the letter, I told him he really didn't need to reply – I needed to write it for myself to get it all out – to let him know some important things on my mind and in my heart. I told her to leave him alone about it.

She didn't.

She said that his non-response was making HER mad and that she was going to talk to him about it.

I told her please don't.

She did anyway.

That seemed to be the second "beginning of the end" of our relationship after he talked to her about my personal letter to him.

AGAIN – she interfered.

Things more significantly weren't the same after that. This time, it was going downhill fast …

LESSONS:

* Learn your partner's preferred communication style and use it.

While you're at it, learn your partner's "Love Language," Zodiac sign, Myers-Briggs Personality Type, Attachment Style … all of it.

Communicating in the way that your partner will understand you and best receive your message is key. Otherwise, you will be talking, texting, writing until you're blue in the face and it will all be a waste – or worse – ruin the relationship altogether, despite your best efforts – just like I did.

* *Desk job or not,* **keep written communication to a minimum**.

* *Most importantly,* **keep deep feelings for in-person conversations**.

These days we do too much texting, messaging, and written communication versus in-person communication, and it's just not working when it comes to emotional connection.

If you care about your partner – truly care about having him/her in your life and care about their happiness and wellbeing – then, you have a responsibility to help them understand what you are trying to say.

So, make your communication count!

P.S. – Mine is song lyrics! If a guy can't write but sends me song lyrics to express his feelings – that's some gold to me right there! But ... that's mine. Find out yours!

Counseling

I'M A FIRM BELIEVER in counseling, always have been, both personal and in marriage.

Counselors don't "fix" anything, but they sure help you clarify thoughts and feelings to empower you to ideally, ultimately "be your own Guru," as I have written about for years now.

Yet, personal counselors cannot possibly be relationship counselors, since they aren't hearing the other side of the story – only what you tell them.

In the case of my dating life and in this particularly challenging situation I was in, my counselor was a blessing and one afternoon in March, she had gotten me to a point where I was finally able to resolve my long-standing insecurities, since the night of the aforementioned breach of "Girl Code" the July prior.

I never thought anything was happening between them currently because I was the one who was involved with him. Yet, I was scared it would happen in the future, because unbeknownst to me at the time, I had serious abandonment issues.

Well, I made the mistake of telling her later that night when we were out ...

I told her that my counselor had finally helped me realize that I can believe what she's been telling me all this time ... that there wasn't any prior "romantic history" between them, and that it wasn't going to happen in the future, because it would have by now.

That should have been the end of it.

But nope ...

Unfortunately, instead of being happy for me and validating that breakthrough in my session, she replied:

> "Well, if that's what you want to believe ... if that's what makes you sleep at night."

Wow. Just. Wow.

That was so cutting, I made a special session the next day, and told my counselor about her reply, and she advised ...

"If everything your friend said prior was true, the correct response should have been, 'Good!'"

Yup. That resonated with me.

That's what I would do for sure! I mean, I do NOT want any of my male friends to like me as any more than a friend.

From my counselor's point of view, her response was toxic and defensive.

She said the response contradicts everything that she's told me thus far about their relationship and it sounds like she WANTED him to be attracted to her, as confirmed in her text below:

> It seems to make you happy drilling it in that he doesn't want me to see if it would hurt me.

See what she said there ... that was absolutely NOT my intention to "hurt her" when I made the comment that night.

I was merely explaining to her that with the help of my counselor, I was finally settled and secure that their relationship never was anything more than friends, isn't now, and never WILL be (i.e., my abandonment issues).

How was me confirming to her that I understood that they were just friends, always were, and always will be "seeing if it would hurt her"?

How was me confirming that I finally believe what she was saying the whole time "seeing if it would hurt her?"

It was supposed to be good news! I wasn't going to say anything more about it! It was supposed to be case closed.

... and look how defensive she got about it!

She WANTED him to want her as more than a friend.

That comment caused MORE issues between her and I – not him. It wasn't his problem. It was between me and HER.

These are the types of comments she would say to me that he never knew, and I couldn't explain to him.

She was like the Warner Brothers Frog cartoon … one way with me and another with him.

He had NO clue that SHE was the one perpetuating this issue by the comments she's said to me in front of our mutual friends, and her reply to this important discussion here … because he was only hearing one side.

She's brilliant. She was using the classic psychological trick of "playing victim to get male attention," as I described in the previous "Girl Code" chapter, playing into his empathy and sexuality as a man to protect her.

Men don't see that … so, he ate it right up.

That said, the conclusion my counselor came up with – and I agree – is that she was secretly jealous of mine and his relationship after all.

For her own sake, I pray she takes a deep look inside her heart and deals with why she was so jealous of my relationship with him before it causes her more suffering with someone else in the future.

LESSON: Your friends are not your counselors. Don't put that burden on them. Keep your own mental and emotional issues between you and your counselor.

Yes, friends often serve as a listening ear or helpful advisor, but when you have serious insecurities, abandonment issues, anxiety, or addiction issues, that's above and beyond what should be expected of your friends to handle. Separate the two.

Jealousy

IT WAS AFTER SHE found out that we were going on that trip together that she started saying those things to upset me. As I mentioned before, it was January when she said the two comments in front of our mutual friends, and February when she interfered in my personal letter to him. March was when she destroyed my progress with my counselor.

I recall once when she and I were out together, she made a huge deal about seeing a girl wearing a jacket with the logo of the bar he frequented. She was SO thrilled, she just HAD to go up to her and have a lengthy conversation all about her friend who goes there asking if she knew him and on and on, and I'm sure she told him all about it.

It seemed to be okay for *her* to bring him up all the time, but then she complained whenever *I* talked about him, saying she was sick of hearing about him and seeing us "making googly eyes" at each other.

Then, I started thinking back and remembered a few other upsetting memories …

We were out one night, and he texted her a picture of himself and his new puppy. She showed me the phone and goes, " Aw, he got a new dog! Look! Gee, I don't know why he had to send me a picture of himself, though?!" … making me wonder why, too …

I mean, I wouldn't have thought anything of it if she hadn't pointed it out, because the puppy was lying on his chest and if I recall, he was looking at the puppy, not really the camera, to take the picture, most likely for size or because it was cute that he was lying on his chest ... I don't understand the purpose of why she had to make it a point to me that he was sending her a picture of *himself*, except perhaps to upset me and try to make me jealous.

In the fall, he came to my house to give me and the kids some of his "award-winning" chili he liked to make each year.

When I told her later, the first thing she said was, "He didn't come give ME any of his chili!"

One day, I got to meet his son, and I made the mistake of telling her, and right away she said, "*I* never got to meet any of his kids!"

It's like she was always comparing. She apparently expected him to treat her the same – if not better – than he treated me.

When I bought her family member flowers in the hospital, he and I agreed they'd be from both of us, so I put both our names on the card. Well, she didn't like that at all. She said she "was confused" why the flowers said they were from both of us. I was irritated that it bothered her so much.

Another time the three of us were out together at a place her daughter worked at the time, and he and I got into a silly argument over a Gwen Stefani song.

71

She sided with him, saying that he was trying to "talk sense" into me. She always sided with him.

In fact, she was always that way, putting her men first even back in the day. That's how we fell off the first time, not by anything bad, but she was too interested in her man at the time and stopped reaching out to me to hang with her.

But, regarding our upcoming trip failing because he couldn't get his passport in time, she said she thought I was being aggressive about asking him to go with me and that he really didn't want to go, because if he really wanted to go, he would make it happen.

> It's not your fault. If he really wanted to go, he would make it happen. I know I did.

> So, you think he really doesn't want to go with me, then?

> I think he does and doesn't – that you are being aggressive with asking him.

See how she always liked to speak for him? … and what an idiot I was, look at that … always depending on HER to tell me what HE thinks. Fool!!!

She said after we broke up that it's probably best, because long-term, she didn't think he was a right "fit" for my family.

All of these "microaggressions" – these subtle, upsetting statements – from her gave me pause.

All this I wanted to tell him, but couldn't …

Never said a word to him. How could I? How would I sound?

For so long, I couldn't understand how they could be "just friends," and then one day it hit me like a ton of bricks …

… it was never HIM I was questioning … HE never said anything to give me pause … it was HER!

The entire time.

That's exactly what my counselor said, too, after I told her about that "If that's what you want to believe," response.

My counselor said that my pain and insecurities didn't come from anything HE has said or done.

He had been solid and consistent this entire time.

It all came from these things that SHE has said!

She said awful things to me because she was jealous.

People who are unhappy with themselves or generally unhappy with their lives don't like to see others win.

It was clearly a case of, "I don't want him (that way), but I don't want anyone else to have him, either."

Or ... maybe she decided she just didn't want ME to have him?

I'm thinking all that time she was supposedly telling him about me to "set us up," was quite a different experience for her actually seeing us together in person and how close we were getting.

I've since realized that the truth is = she honestly didn't expect I'd be interested in him.

In the beginning she told me "Just have fun with him!"

My feelings for him came as a total surprise to her, and she didn't like it.

She told me once that when she was around us, she felt like a third wheel. Well, duh! I mean, she was! We were on dates that she shouldn't've been! It should NEVER have been the three of us hanging out in a new relationship like we did.

I blame myself for not setting that boundary, but I was scared of how I'd come across and lose him.

I wonder if she felt like a "third wheel" around his previous girlfriends, too?

So, since she'd always say these upsetting things to me, making me over-think, when I asked her to explain how they could be so close and "best friends," everything that came out of her mouth just always made it worse.

"We're just like brother and sister! … Except brothers and sisters don't do what we did …" she quipped.

Nice. Real nice.

She loved to constantly remind me that she'd known him longer than me, been friends with him longer than me, and that he'd "do anything" for her.

She'd say, "He never fails me."

"He is my 'go-to' guy."

"I like men who are handy who could do things around the house for me."

(He had put her living room floor and kitchen tile in for her in her new house.)

"He and I will always be just fine."

(She said this one in response to me telling her I hoped they would be able to patch up a serious argument they had about politics, because I said it'd be a shame to lose a friend for so many years over that.)

She was very smug about their relationship.

… As if she knew she had him in the palm of her hand.

She really made it seem like she'd say "Jump!," and he'd be like "How high? And what can I get you while I'm up there?"

Like, he was her third dog.

I mean, he WAS rather helpful to her in the months I've witnessed, such as all that work on her new house – quite a bit above and beyond "just a friend."

It made me wonder … what did she do to gain this kind of blind loyalty?

Did she save his life?

Did she have some kind of dirt on him?

Once, I did attempt to ask him about their relationship dynamic, seeing what his thoughts were. He simply replied, "She's my sister." Case closed.

That made sense to me, because I've witnessed many times her telling him what to do, giving him advice.

I think she did her best to give him a woman's perspective on things and really try and help him become a better man, and help him in his own life, and get his help in return when needed.

In fact, she told me it was her idea for him to pick me up at O'Hare from that vacation he couldn't join me on, for instance.

She's a few years older than us (I'm one year younger than him), so I observed that he seems to view her as his "big sister," and it's possible that she may perhaps view him as her "little brother," since she has two older ones already, and she is the youngest, so she has no younger siblings. Maybe that's what he and I were to her?

It seemed to me as though despite what happened between them, he "friend-zoned" her decades ago.

His answer resonated with me – it "felt right." That was the end of the story for him. I believed that was the case, and I never asked him about it again.

Now HER, on the other hand … she'd constantly brag that their relationship was "special" and "rare" and he's "like family," and that her parents consider him their "third son," and that her kids called him "Uncle" …

So, did she ever stop to think for one minute that ANY of that was a good idea to tell me?

… that ANY of that was supposed to make me feel secure in my new relationship with him?

When I heard all that, I was jealous, too!

My mind was spinning again with the insecure, anxious thoughts …

How was I EVER supposed to compete with that?

Where does a woman stand with him, when he's already got that kind of emotional intimacy with HER?

What was *I* to him then ... just a piece of @$$, that he wasn't getting from HER?

I felt like SHE was his wife, and I was his mistress.

I clearly recall another evening when all three of us were out together at the same place as our first date, but a week or two after, we were about to leave, so I went to the bathroom.

When I came back to the table, I found the two of them with tears in their eyes and wiping them ...

What did I miss??

What the heck is going on here??? ...

Well, I found out she had just told him of her first serious health concern that she had just learned about and her fears around it.

I recognize an important emotional moment between two people when I see it ...

And I knew I was not a part of this moment between them, and that I needed to leave.

And so, I did.

That hit me hard.

I knew there was a bond there I didn't have ....

At least not yet.

My self-defeating talk told me that I NEVER would, and that I NEVER possibly could …

30+ years between them …

I was literally sick to my stomach, and a wellspring of emotion came upon me.

It was a horrible feeling seeing them two together like that … almost like I had caught them in bed.

… and then I felt guilty for feeling that way!

I needed to leave right away, and he was going to walk me to my car, but I told him to just walk her to hers.

I couldn't handle that kind of emotional bond they had together – but felt awful thinking that, since she was in a bad way and needed all the support she could get.

We were newly dating, and it was all too much.

I was the third wheel! (I decided.)

I was the one who didn't belong.

I was completely torn.

I had to think …

Once I got outside, the tears came streaming down, and I couldn't stop them.

My mind was screaming …

I was NOT ready for this relationship.

Something was off here ...

He ran outside to me on the driver's side of my car, but I couldn't even explain it to him – all these thoughts in my head.

I told him just to go walk her to her car, that she needed him more than me right now.

He said he could see her anytime, but that he came there that night to see ME.

Well, that was another heartwarming thing to say to me, but my mind and emotions were screaming that something wasn't right in this situation.

I needed to understand their relationship better to fully know what was going on between them.

I foolishly disregarded my feelings.

I swept them under the rug and continued the relationship.

... trying to be "strong" and "cool" about them being "just friends" ...

Uh-huh ...

If I could go back, I would have stopped seeing him until I figured my own stuff out and figured out why I had that kind of visceral reaction to seeing them like that.

In hindsight, I am impressed that he is the type of man capable of having "just a friendship" with a woman.

I never said or did anything to try and mess that up, and I had NO intention of doing so.

If anything, I always took a step back time and time again, as described above.

The epiphany I had many months later after this incident was simply that it was the "emotional intimacy" between the two of them that was hurting me – because it's what I didn't feel I had with him yet.

It never occurred to me at the time that – yes – I COULD achieve that with him, too, over time, and that the years between the two relationships are not what matters …

It's the quality of the connection that matters.

Same as with people who stay married 30 plus years who can't stand each other but can feel more emotionally connected to people they've met in only a matter of months.

I get it now!

(Over 2 years later, as of this writing!)

I remember a few times in the beginning she was trying to help me, telling me when I was in the midst of my insecurities that I should have more self-confidence.

I told her that I did, but I see now that I really didn't.

I get it now!

Much later in my healing journey, I heard something in one of Matthew Hussey's videos that further drove this point home for me. He said:

"Romantic love fills different spaces in our heart."

That's why I could have been valuable to him, too, besides her.

I get it now!

Unfortunately, however, this episode was only a dark precursor of the worst of what she would say and do to me to continue to trigger those old insecurities and past trauma.

We are only human, and sometimes even people you've known for decades tend to put their own needs first – even those who you thought had your back. It is human nature … especially in the realm of romantic relationships.

LESSONS:

* Jealousy stems from insecurity.

* I had no business and no right to unleash all my insecurities onto either one of them. It was my own personal problem, and I should have dealt with it myself – via my counselor, far-removed friends, my Prayer Ministry, journaling, praying, etc., anything but spewing onto them like I did.

* The moment I noticed her jealous comments, I should have immediately protected my relationship with him from her

and stopped talking about him to her. Jealousy has no place in a healthy relationship — romantic, friendship, business, or otherwise.

* People can achieve emotional intimacy over time.

* The number of years in a relationship is not what matters — it's the quality of the connection that matters.

The Final Argument

I AM A BIG fan of our local Chicagoland morning show called "The Fred Show" on 103.5 WKSC "Kiss-FM." In particular, I love their "Waiting by the Phone" segment, because I find the stories so interesting.

The premise of this segment is that folks go on first dates, and then they never get a second date – they get "ghosted," which means the person never returns any of their calls or messages and they never hear from the date again. The "ghostee" calls Fred and gives him the date's phone number to see if he can call them to find out what happened.

Coincidentally one Wednesday morning after Mother's Day, the subject of the segment centered around the same situation I was in with her but reversed between guys = this guy was set up by his buddy with a girl, and they went out on a date, and he found out during the course of the conversation that she slept with his buddy who set them up, but his buddy didn't disclose that beforehand.

Well, he was upset that his friend broke "Bro Code," which means that before setting someone up with someone else, the "code" is that the person discloses if they've had a sexual relationship with them.

The trust was broken.

Because now I had a solid example of how my situation made me feel with her, I sent the audio segment to her in the hopes she would finally understand my perspective and apologize.

Finally, she did!

That night, she FINALLY apologized after all this time!

... after ALL those months of making excuses, and dismissing my feelings, and telling me how it "meant nothing," "if anything, it was just a hookup," "I was drunk," "we were both drinking," "my other friends wouldn't've' cared" and so on, blah, blah, blah ...

That night, she FINALLY honored my feelings and apologized!

She said, "I'm sorry that I didn't tell you beforehand! Are you happy now? Is that what you want to hear?"

... and I forgave her.

Once again, that should have been the end of it.

But nope ...

Unfortunately, in her very next breath, she dropped this bomb on me ... she goes ...

"Well, you know I asked him.

Confused, I reply, "Asked him what?"

"I asked him if he would sleep with me."

And, I got really REALLY upset, since he and I were still involved.

I asked, "Okay ... when was this?"

And she proceeds to describe the exact time she asked him ... which ended up being over TWO months prior while driving him to a family gathering! (The event was early March and it was now mid-May.)

I was absolutely livid.

AGAIN, she kept information from me all this time!

Obviously, I ask, "Okay, well, what did he say?"

"He said no."

And I'm like, "Okay ..."

And then she prods me with, "Well, what if he said yes?"

And I got even MORE upset ...

She continued to press me, "WELL, what IF he said yes ...? THEN what would you think???"

She was clearly egging me on to say something ...

And that's when I completely blew my fuse and I yelled, "Well, F#@+, if he said YES, and that's the CASE, then it would be MY F#@+-ing luck, and I WOULDN'T be surprised!!!!"

And she then got up and walked away.

It was a ridiculous question!

Why SHOULDN'T I be surprised? ... "Friends" fall in love all the time! It was my biggest fear this whole time! It WOULD be just my luck!!!

And, I mean, if he said "yes," then it's a done deal, that means he's into her, and I'm dust.

And I'm well aware that sex to her is "No big deal," as she told me months earlier.

Well, I don't feel that way. At all.

My sexual values and relationship values are vastly different from hers.

THAT is why I said I wouldn't be surprised.

Because I know her. I know how she is.

The way I felt in that moment, after all she's said to me and in front of our friends, I wholeheartedly believed that if he ever said "Yes," that she would in a heartbeat.

In fact, based on all her comments she's made all this time, I wouldn't be surprised if SHE was the one who initiated it with him the time that it DID happen between them in the first place!

I never asked that question, although I'm curious to know if I'm right, which I'm sure I am, because she said that she thought back then the "roles were reversed," whatever that means ...

Why in God's name would she ask him a question like that if she viewed him as "just a friend"? Friends just don't "go there" on that subject – especially when they are involved with someone else. How inappropriate with him and disrespectful to me!

She told me that she blamed ME for HER asking him, saying that *I* wouldn't stop talking about it.

… and then she had the nerve to get mad at ME for my answer to her "What if he said yes" question?

I mean … WTH kind of game is that???

Anyway, she was dead wrong, I had specifically made it a point NOT to talk to her about him for months … ever since that disaster night I told her about my progress with my counselor.

I ONLY brought this up now because of the coincidence of the radio show I heard that morning, hoping to get an apology out of her after almost a YEAR later … which I FINALLY did …

But was it worth it?

No …

… because she'd simply continue to hurt and betray me even worse going forward.

She got EXACLY what she wanted.

She got me to say what I said, so that she could run and tell him.

And he foolishly took it in without any context, and immediately hated me for it, because he'd already been blindly "seeded" by her for months.

And believe it or not, I was STILL trying to hang onto to her after this episode ... STILL foolishly believing that she was my friend ... STILL trying my best to practice compassion for her situation and help her.

LESSONS:

* If there is something you need from someone in a relationship – be it an apology or an explanation – make that request as soon as you can.

* Do NOT ignore your needs. Do NOT sweep them under the rug to let it fester for months on end, like I did.

If something hits you hard, take a pause, breathe, work through the feeling, figure out what is going on inside of you and WHY it's hitting you so hard.

It's important to get that answer and resolve it before choosing to continue with the relationship, because otherwise, it will fester and keep presenting itself until it is resolved.

All I wanted was for her to understand and empathize with my feelings and for her to apologize for her breach of trust. Had I simply told her that I needed her to understand how much her keeping that a secret hurt me and that I needed an apology, perhaps that would have helped. Had I just requested that of her soon after I found out the news, processed it properly, and decided how I needed to proceed with the relationship right then, it never would have gotten to this point.

This is how I disrespected my own needs.

Don't ever do that to yourself.

The Ghosting

So, AFTER THAT ARGUMENT, she and I argued some more the following days via Facebook Messenger.

She messaged me some awful stuff and it got out of hand. So, I just took a screen shot, deleted the entire conversation, and figured I'd just read it another time if I wanted, because I was just SO done with this.

I did not send her that radio show audio to start all of this. I sent it to her to try and regain some kind of trust with her, which completely failed, because she once again made things ten times worse with her response.

Anyway, there were other things going on that were more important than this. She had serious, potentially life-threatening issues to deal with, on top of just going through the nightmare of losing a close family member – and thus, was the main reason why I remained her friend, choosing to put aside everything she's done to me up until then, and fought so hard to salvage our friendship, despite what was happening with this guy she introduced me to.

I figured, romantic relationships come and go, but friendship is supposed to be forever … right???

So, we made up again. That's what friends do, right???

It was a moot point, anyway, because he wasn't even around anymore – he got a job out of state, so he was gone indefinitely, although we were still "involved" from a distance, messaging each other and such.

In fact, he was just here visiting for Mother's Day weekend – the weekend prior to our argument – he gave me an incredibly thoughtful gift and got to meet my kids in person for the first time (he already "met" my daughter "virtually" over the holidays).

I was excited that we had just made plans for me to drive out for a visit when he was in a nearby state in the next week or two, since it was only a couple hours' drive and I love driving.

The kicker is that just before he started this job, we talked about a second chance for us. We both agreed we deserved it.

> Hopefully, we get another chance someday.
> We deserve it.

We do.

> I'm really glad you found me … pursued me.

The feeling is mutual.

Unfortunately, however, we also both agreed that now was not the time, because he didn't know what his new schedule in this job was going to be like.

He knew I wanted a man with me on a regular, permanent basis – to be a part of my day-to-day life – to do all the activities we enjoyed together, and to plan things with.

However, he needed this opportunity to do some things in his life that the pandemic had ruined for him, and so now, he simply wasn't in a place for that kind of relationship with me anymore. I was very clear about that – I totally understood and respected his decision.

This exchange I believe was sometime in January:

> I miss being "your woman," … sometimes, LOL!

> LOL, probably for the best right now since I'm very unhappy with how things are going for me. I'm angry too often and that's not fair to others.

I understand. You gotta get things right again with yourself. I am making strides on doing the same for myself, too.

I really do. I can't stand living this kind of life.

At the end of March, just before he left, we again talked about making it "official," since we never stopped seeing each other since we "broke up," and we weren't dating anyone else.

I remember that day at his place. I told him that I'd like to have an exclusive relationship with him again and he smiled said, "Well, I'M not seeing anyone else!"

Then, I looked him directly in the eyes and told him that she was telling me to let him go and to move on and to leave him alone and I asked him point blank if that is what I should do …

He shook his head and said, "I would love to tell you no, but I don't know what this job will entail."

He didn't quite know the travel schedule, but we knew for sure it would be months at a time that he'd be gone – and said that "it wouldn't be fair to me," so, the last thing he said to me in person before he left to start was ...

"Things will be better once I get this job."

I thought that meant he just had to get settled in this job and whatever he wanted in his life straightened out, and then we could be together again and give it a real shot between us this time.

I was looking forward to that day when we would change our relationship status back to "in a relationship with" each other again on Facebook with our cute matching profile pictures to let everyone in our lives know that we were starting over, better, stronger, being supported by the people we love and care about who care for us and would be happy for us, like when we did that the first time.

Doing that was important to me, because I didn't mean it like I was just "showing off" that I was in a relationship – I was proud of him. I really liked him. I wanted everyone I knew to know him, too.

To me, changing our relationship status on social media showed each other that – how proud we were of each other, and let anyone know who was interested in us as any more than a friend that we were officially off the market! No more "Situationship" – this one is for real!

Until then, for me, the "conflict" in my heart with her was over – she finally apologized! She finally understood how she hurt me.

And now, he's gone on this job, so she didn't have to see or hear about us together anymore … and he and I weren't officially "together," anyway – just like she wanted – so, she was happy.

However, as I was coordinating our upcoming season in the team we were on, we all decided to get team t-shirts and tanks this year, and he bought one.

In fact, he designed it.

He was in touch with me every step of the way in designing and ordering the team t-shirts/tanks. He was even asking a friend of his who was in printing, but he was so busy with his new job, and he didn't hear back from his friend in time, so I found something local.

He bought a tank because he was still hoping to play whenever he was in town.

So, I was really hoping (expecting) that would happen.

Also, we made a deal with each other that when he got his motorcycle fixed, I would fight my fear and allow him to finally take me on it for my first ride since my uncle's motorcycle when I was a teenager!

When I told him how scared I was, he joked, "Don't worry, I'll wrap you up in bubble wrap!"

And if I was alright with riding on it, we'd plan his road trip idea that he wanted to take me on which he told me about in the beginning, visiting restaurants he liked.

I would have loved it!

I love to travel and try new things.

In the meantime, we maintained the agreement that we were not in an exclusive, committed relationship since we talked about it a few months prior, as I mentioned – therefore, we were both free to do what we needed to do in our lives right now.

But, as you can see, we fully planned to see each other again whenever he was back in town and make the most of it when we did.

It was my understanding that we were simply keeping in touch and seeing each other whenever we could – continuing our "Situationship" on an even more distant, casual basis, purely because of this job – definitely not because our feelings for each other weren't there (at least not for me) … and that's just the way it had to be, for now.

I was completely unprepared for what was to come.

That following Tuesday evening of my argument with her, he video called me, like he always did, and I was so happy to hear from him twice in the same day!

I was just on a video call with him earlier that afternoon, because he was helping me install my blinds in my bedroom. It was my first time doing that, and even at a distance, he offered to help me as always, and I was so touched.

Well, I wish I had never taken the call this time.

It was nighttime now and dark, and he was driving home from out of state only overnight for an appointment in the morning, so the signal was choppy. He kept cutting out and I could barely even see his face to try and make out what he was saying.

He must have just gotten off the phone with her, because this time angrily started out with, "So I hear you and she are fighting again ..."

I said, "What do you mean?"

I asked that because, as I mentioned, we had already made up by then, and because he didn't hear that from ME, he only heard it from HER.

I never told him ANY of my conflicts I had with her, because it was between me and HER – it was not a problem with him.

I didn't make it a practice to tell him things I knew would upset him for no reason at all.

I'm not stupid!

I'm not ignorant like that.

He said "Listen, her and I have known each other for 30 years, there's not much I don't know ..."

That statement said it all.

He told me right then that there was nothing ever personal or sacred between him and I.

"Knowing each other 30 years" and she "tells him everything" – he said it RIGHT there …

… she was right in the middle of our relationship telling him "everything" about me and telling ME "everything" about him.

Our relationship all along was me, him, and her.

He said the word "again" ... that we were fighting "again."

THAT is a statement that speaks volumes in and of itself = the fact that she told him things behind my back giving him only HER side and the other is that word "again," meaning she's said these things to him at least more than once – really, I will never know how many times.

I know for a FACT that *I* never told him about our discussions, because they were between me and HER, and had nothing to do with him.

Since he'd been gone, it seemed to me that everything was fine between us until just then.

I had NO problem with him.

And I certainly didn't want to upset him in his new job with issues that didn't have anything to do with him.

So ... he got his information from only one other source = her.

She was in the middle of us – it's what I ONCE tried to tell him was happening ALL along.

He continued his angry rant, going on to say that I was "twisting things," and that I had "alcohol muscles," but didn't tell me what he was so upset about.

If he did, I didn't hear it, because as I said, he kept cutting off and I couldn't make out what he was saying.

Then, he said, "You're a smart, successful woman ... why don't you get this?" but he didn't tell me what "this" was.

He said I was "scaring" him, but he didn't tell me why.

He said, "If this were 10 years ago, I'd ..." and then cut off again.

THAT is where I got freaked out and asked him about that deeply personal thing that she said about his past back in late January in front of that mutual friend at dinner to prove that she was also talking about HIM to ME as well.

He admitted it but said that was long ago.

Then, I told him about how she told us that his special nickname for her was "Sweetheart."

He replied, "No, it's not a 'special nickname,' it's just a term of endearment – I call many women 'Sweetheart.' I only call YOU 'Honey'."

Which was totally true. He did call me that. And I absolutely loved it when he did.

My maternal grandparents used to only call each other "Hon." In my entire life, I never heard them call each other by their first names – ever.

I had a special nickname for him, too, which I will not disclose here.

He didn't say, "I USED to call you 'Honey,'" or "I CALLED you 'Honey.'" He said, "I CALL you 'Honey.'"

I was still his "Honey" on that phone call.

But then my phone died, so I hopped on the computer to call him back (we were on Facebook Messenger), but by then, he arrived at his house, got his mail, played with his dog, and then HIS phone died.

We never got to finish our conversation.

But he was already convinced of whatever he heard from her, anyways.

His mind was already made up.

He didn't want to listen to a word I said.

I had NO chance.

That call was NOT a good experience for me at all – it was very attacking.

He made me cry.

Over the next day, he messaged me mysterious platitudes about friendship, such as "'friends' are supposed to be 'friendly' towards each other" and that "'friends' aren't supposed to 'pour gas on it and see if a firework will set it off.'"

Ironically, months earlier when I asked him about something I heard from her, he told me, "If someone says something about me without me knowing, it's probably not accurate," but here … he never gave ME the same courtesy.

Then, he told me I apparently said or did something "inappropriate" to her daughter, but he never told me what it was.

Again, I was kept in the dark, completely confused and upset.

Well, at least things seemed to be fine with me and her at the moment, so I decided to pull up those screenshots of the messages I deleted a few days earlier to see if I could figure out what he was talking about.

What a HUGE mistake!

It was brutal, and made me feel ten times worse …

... so, sometimes we say s*** that we don't really mean that yeah maybe just to piss you off or to irritate you.

"Whatever lets you sleep at night." I'm really done with this.

I made a HUGE mistake introducing you two. I told him the same. I regret it.

I do agree that some of the things I say are mean, but you know what, that's my nature. You do things your way and I'll do things my way.

My biggest mistake was introducing the two of you. And for that, I am tremendously sorry.

So, on top of everything, now she's saying that they regularly collaborate to purposely say things to upset me.

Knife. In. Back.

This was a betrayal unlike anything I've ever experienced in my entire life.

I was absolutely devastated.

Now, I had no idea exactly when this collaboration started ... how long had it been going on, I wondered?

I was so angry, I blocked him from Messenger that very night.

It was a Thursday night, and I had a busy day the next day and figured blocking him would show him how upset I was, and it would give me some space and time to think about what was happening here with her message, and that I'd get back to him later when I could.

I just didn't want to see his face on my phone any longer.

The next morning (now Friday), I left her a tearful audio message and relayed to her the conversation on his video call that he and I had a few days' prior and giving her a piece of my mind about how I felt about her going behind my back like this to the person – yes – whom SHE introduced me to, but WE had a relationship going.

She had NO business interfering like she did.

It was unbelievably cruel.

Later that night, after I had cooled down, I went to unblock him, but he was gone.

He had unfriended me on Facebook.

This was Friday, May 20th, 2022.

The next morning, Saturday, I sent him a text apologizing for blocking him and said I just needed the time to cool down and that I needed to talk to him.

I wanted to tell him about the message I had read and find out what was going on with this unfriending business.

No reply.

The next day, Sunday, I called and left a voice mail.

No reply.

The "ghosting" had begun.

I only received one final text about paying for his team t-shirt.

And two other messages about her surgery on July 1, 2022, because she asked him to be there for her.

She had at least 5 other family members she could have had with her. I couldn't because I had my kids.

He was working in Texas at the time, so that means he drove over 15 hours to be by her side. If that's not love, I don't know what is. She's a lucky woman!

I had been sending him several messages on Facebook Messenger throughout June.

He would read them all, but never reply.

Then, I texted him a month or so later telling him our team won and made it to the playoffs, and I actually got a response on that one:

> That's awesome. Tell everyone I said great job and good luck. Win some more

And that was the very last message he ever sent me.

I've never heard from him since.

I stopped texting or messaging him, but I sent him an email that September for some kind of closure on my end, although I have no idea if he read it.

Our plans to meet – gone.

His gift to me – a painful souvenir.

Our 10-month involvement – done.

He threw me out of his life like a piece of garbage.

No explanation.

No discussion.

No reason.

LESSONS:

* Never allow a conversation to proceed when it crosses the boundary of insults, name-calling, referencing third-party information, or even a bad digital connection. End the conversation immediately until you get a better connection, get more information from the third-party, and most importantly, until the person is calm enough to talk to you respectfully, like a rational adult.

Nothing productive will ever come from continuing to engage with the person and will only make it worse. Folks need to cool down and be in a relatively calm state in order to communicate productively, so learn to say something along the lines of, "Let's talk at a later time when 1. we have a better signal, or 2. when we are both cooled down, or 3. when I can get more information."

* You never know when the last time will be that you talk to someone. Don't block people out of anger in the moment. Make sure you keep the conversation going to resolve things. We can't always depend on tomorrow.

Alcohol

I MUST ADDRESS WHAT he said to me about having "alcohol muscles."

He was sensitive on the issue, because he told me that all his exes were big drinkers and could not go a day without drinking, and that's why he was so impressed with me that I only drank on the days that I didn't have my kids and about the long breaks I went on, on top of how I worked out and took care of myself every day.

That's why I was so hurt and confused by this insult from him, and so very surprised at how he could be so sure of my condition when he wasn't even there.

It says a lot about his character to make assumptions like that, and how blindly he trusted her over me.

He obviously didn't consider that between girlfriends – same as guy friends – we drink socially as a bonding time to share and have deep conversations.

She and I were out socially both times we had these arguments, and yes, we BOTH had drinks.

I thought I was in a "safe space" to have a deep conversation with my "best friend" and discuss important topics with her that were on my mind and in my heart.

Again, the "Girl Code" is that our personal conversations are to be kept between us girls.

Unfortunately, as I learned the hard way, that simply was not the case with her, since she has no "Girl Code."

What's also interesting is that the times in January she made comments in front of our mutual friends, I didn't have a drop to drink, because I was doing "Dry January" again that year.

So, alcohol wasn't even a factor those times, and she STILL had an issue with me ... my "best friend."

If you find yourself in a relationship where you tend to end up in arguments when one or both of you are drinking, it's a huge red flag.

Alcohol is prevalent in our society today, and nice to enjoy in moderation. Unfortunately, it just gets to be too much at times and can ruin relationships. It unfortunately played a role in my having to get divorced.

Also, case in point of "the breakup." That was my mistake at the concert that night, getting so depressed and over-thinking. I 100% own that.

Yes, during the worse times of this painful ordeal, I had gotten despondent like that, and hurt myself a few times.

I discovered that I could lose track when I'm not careful and heartbroken. I identified that in the past, I drank to cope with what was going on, because I was angry and upset and wanted to numb myself – both through my divorce and in this horrific situation.

That's exactly why I take breaks. I've taken Dry January, my own made-up "AF April", another made-up "Attune June," Sober October, and such, whenever I want. Not only is it a healthy thing to do but saves me tons of money! I only drink half the time anyway because I never drink when I have my kids, so it's no big deal for me.

Also, I discovered a Facebook group called "The Mindful Drinkers – Cutting Back Together," and I have shared that page with friends. I look out for them, too, and I'm so incredibly appreciative when they look out for me.

If needed, all they need to do is ask me how many I've had, and that's my cue. That shows me they care, and I'm forever grateful. Those are good friends. Those are the keepers. I do that for them as well, if needed.

For instance, it would have been impressive the night of the breakup instead of walking out on me, if he would have come by me and asked me if I was alright – and if he determined I was not, to say something like, "Honey, I think it's time for us to leave," and put his arm around me and we both leave together.

That's a real man! That simple act would have changed everything.

The man for me can be trusted when we're drinking together – he will know if I've had too much and if we should talk another time. He'd be a wise gentleman and know my character.

On a first date with a man I've only recently met, I prefer not to have any alcohol.

My Mom doesn't drink, and I have several friends who quit. A few have been sober for several years, and a few have only recently joined that trend, as it's becoming more and more popular due to the increased availability of non-alcoholic beers and wines being made, and "mocktails" for those of us who do Dry January and other breaks.

It's also becoming more popular now that cannabis has become legalized. Many of my non-drinking friends are strictly "sober," while a few never drink alcohol, but instead partake in "nature's medicine." A friend of mine taught me the name for that option is called "California Sober."

Bottom line is that I have added this chapter because it's important. If you feel you have an uncomfortable or unhealthy relationship with alcohol, please get help.

LESSON: Make sure alcohol isn't ruining your relationships. It's important to decide what role, if any, alcohol plays in your relationship, because it impairs your thinking, and can cause problems if not in check.

The Aftermath

"GHOSTING" SOMEONE WHO CARES for you and who is trying to communicate with you is a form of sadistic torture.

As I mentioned in the last chapter, I was reaching out to him on Facebook Messenger, trying to figure out what happened, and he would read my messages, but never reply ... not even "react" ... not even to tell me to stop messaging him ... never even blocked me.

It was inhumane.

The very definition of selfish.

And, beyond cruel.

Without hearing someone's own words, we "fill in" the information ourselves and typically write a narrative about what happened that may or may not be true, because we need to complete the story.

It was a horribly destructive experience for me and took me an enormous amount of time and effort to have some sort of "recovery."

Thus, I have healed enough now and had enough time pass for me to be able to write this book to process what happened and help others avoid this kind of tragedy.

He acted like a coward.

He lacked the courage to have a tough conversation with me, and in doing so, it destroyed my confidence and my heart.

It was a roller coaster ride of emotions that affected me both mentally and physically.

It completely broke me.

I'm thinking that it's likely I lost about 3-5 years of my life during this past year and a half (as of this writing), considering all the physical and mental damage done from the stress and pain of being ghosted in this way.

… being led on with the idea of a future and plans

… then being verbally attacked due to words he heard from my "best friend"

… and then silence

… not even being given the human decency to respond

… not even given a reason for the silence.

When he came to give me his touching, personalized Mother's Day gift and meet my kids in person for the first time, I really thought that it was serious now.

I really thought that showed he really meant what he said that "things will be better once he gets this job," and that he had a plan, and that he would really come back and see me when he could just like that and possibly make a game, like he said he wanted to, since he bought a team tank and all.

I was so excited!

His actions seemed to be showing me he was for real – just like his many actions had been showing me all along – for months.

It was completely devastating when he cut me out of his life entirely the very next week ...

... after a phone call from her.

She ruined us.

And, I don't even know for how long she'd been doing this.

Behind my back.

When, I'd been there for her throughout everything, doing anything and everything I could.

But thank goodness, I'm an extremely strong person, so I picked myself up and continue to do so every day.

I was desperate to figure out what happened and resolve this, so I stopped trying with him and instead went to her for help.

She was happy now, since she wanted us separated for quite some time (since February – that's when she first told us she regretted us after my letter, but who knows, it could have been sooner that she was feeling that way?).

I asked her, "What did you say to him?" I wanted to know what he meant that she told him we were "fighting again."

Unfortunately, she kept denying that she had told him anything.

She insisted that he "ghosted" me of his own accord and that his decision had nothing to do with anything she told him whatsoever.

The one thing she did say one night as we were walking to our cars after an event was that the reason them two stopped talking for a couple of weeks after he "ghosted" me was because "There was something we both weren't supposed to tell you."

Wow.

More collaborating behind my back against me.

What a punch in the throat!

Afterward, she kept encouraging me to "just move on," and "find someone else," saying that there's someone so much better for me out there.

That was supportive of her and kind to say, but it wasn't what I was ready to hear just then, because at that time, I wasn't interested in finding anyone else. I don't operate that way. I'm a one-man woman. Always have been.

She once said she thought I was the best of all his girlfriends, which warmed my heart!

She said she introduced us because she thought we were perfect for each other, and so I pleaded with her to help us.

> If what you said is true and you really do think we're perfect for each other, then help us! Please.

> That was then. I don't think he's worth your tears and frustration.
> There is a guy who won't do this to you. I can try to heal you guys, but the rest will be between you two.

I got a real kick out of that one ...

So, NOW "the rest is up to us," huh? It would have been nice if that were the case all along.

She went on to try and make me feel better ...

> I believe there is a better man for you who won't make you feel this way. A "Godly" man at that.

> God put him in your
> path for a reason, and
> had me introduce u at a
> time for a reason.

> So, let the reason be,
> take the knowledge, the
> feelings, all of it and
> move on. I am.

Wow! How nice that SHE could move on! …

She then told me she DID talk to him, but that he wouldn't tell her the reason either except that I had "3 Strikes."

He's a huge baseball fan, so apparently, he's got a game called "3 Strikes" he plays with women. He secretly keeps score of their "mistakes" and ghosts them when they've done the third "mistake."

So, he really did me a favor here, because that is not a man capable of ever having a lifelong relationship.

Anything could set him off at any point for any reason.

He had this planned all along; it was just a matter of time.

I never had a chance with him, and I didn't even know it.

He never communicated to me that I was being kept score on – only to her.

He would tell HER things he didn't like about me (as in her comment about me being "too happy") but he wasn't telling ME.

So much for "we'll be fine as long as we communicate."

Our relationship was doomed from the start with that attitude – and by him talking to HER about our relationship and not talking to ME.

I'm looking to be in a healthy, thriving relationship where there's communication and human empathy, at the very least. One where there's give-and-take, respect, loyalty – all that a mutually-fulfilling relationship requires.

Instead, he allowed my "best friend" to share with him my personal conversations I had with her behind my back that had nothing to do with him, then he had the audacity and hypocrisy to turn around and give ME a lecture on "friendship," after everything I've done for her, and he sat there and witnessed her betraying me to him left and right and was blind to all that …

… not to mention that she told each of us to our faces that she regretted introducing us, and thus, she had a vested interest in seeing us apart.

He chose the relationship he wanted to maintain.

He left me in the dust.

Without any regard for my feelings whatsoever.

Yet, he chose to take as gold every single word she said to him about me.

We had been romantically involved for 10 months and then he cut me out of his life with NO explanation ... based solely on what SHE was saying to him about me and nothing more.

He ran away, like "an angry teenager."

He wasn't even there during the conversations between me and her.

He had NO clue how it all went down or why.

Funny, he didn't even consider that all the talking she was doing behind my back to him about me ... she was doing the SAME thing to ME about HIM.

I could write an entire chapter about criticisms she had about him throughout!

The difference is – I didn't let it affect how I felt for him as a person.

I have my own mind, and I don't let others influence me.

I go straight to the source if I have an issue with someone.

I had no issue with him.

I was crystal clear that mine and his relationship was technically defined as "casual" for several months now.

Problem is, he and I had conversations since then that I interpreted otherwise.

I thought he really cared for me like I cared for him.

I thought once he got his life the way he wanted it, that we'd be able to try again.

Well, apparently, I was wrong.

Instead, I discovered from her that they both had a game of purposely saying things to "poke the bear" in an alliance with her to hurt me in some kind of sick game they were playing against me, which was quite the blow.

THAT is why I blocked him on Messenger that night after I read her message. When I saw those words in her message, "He and I say things yeah to upset you ..." I snapped.

It was just too much.

It was just too devastating for me to handle.

That statement was clearly saying they collaborated in that game – that she knew what HE was saying to me to make me upset, and he knew what SHE was saying to me to purposely set me off, and then both turn around to point the finger at me and be upset that *I* was upset.

That's really low and twisted.

I thought he said friends didn't do that.

He is not the man I thought he was.

I have NO idea who he is anymore.

He operated on one side of a story with false and half-information.

There's SO MUCH he didn't know ...

He made a H-U-G-E mistake.

I'm just really surprised that in all those months that she was going behind my back and telling him things I supposedly said and whatever other stuff she said about me that at no point any of it disgusted him in the least.

Like, he's sitting there giving ME a lecture about friendship and how a friend should act, but here he was entertaining all this talking about me to him from my "best friend" ... to the man SHE set me up with, who I was involved with, and who she knew full well I was crazy about and wanted to possibly explore a future with, but sitting there ACTIVELY ruining my relationship with him instead.

Apparently, that was A-OK with him.

Apparently, he didn't see how messed up that was for her to do to me, and for him to allow that to happen and to take her side no questions asked – like a puppet – running to him every time her and I had words.

Instead of coming back to me to verify if it was true, he just blindly took her word and didn't even consider what she was doing to her so-called "best friend".

I thought he was smarter than that.

It's interesting that he never asked me my side at all – never asked me what started those arguments we had and especially what started the one that he came back to yell at me about.

His anger directly stemmed from everything he was hearing from her ... for Lord knows how long.

The facts are:

- She proved that her loyalty lies with him over me.

- She shared our private conversations with him.

- She purposefully said things to hurt me in alliance with him.

- She's proven that my name isn't safe in her mouth to him, and now he hates me for it.

- She's poisoned mine and his relationship with her involvement, instead of supporting it.

The whole thing comes down to lack of communication.

It's the #1 reason relationships are destroyed.

In hindsight, I should have forwarded him her message right then and asked HIM directly if it was true or not before I cut him off on Messenger for the day.

I know now that I will never do that to someone I care about ever again.

No matter how angry I get – I will ask THEM first and hear what THEY have to say, because that's the right thing to do – the emotionally mature thing to do.

On his end, she could have told him anything at all, but if he cared about me and our relationship, he would have come back to ME to discuss.

But he didn't.

So, the way I see it, yes, she betrayed my trust and got in between us, but it was up to him and me to talk to each other and we just didn't.

In this situation, he had a decision to make:

1. Listen to his heart, or
2. Listen to her filter.

He chose the latter.

I take ownership for my part in not telling him the things that she was saying that I should have.

But he always liked to brag about how close they were, so I had a gut feeling he'd not want to listen to anything I had to say and take her side – and I was right.

He proved me right about him.

It's just interesting that their whole reasoning behind them saying these things to upset me was in retaliation that I was simply struggling to understand their relationship, and that is all.

I understand now that when I kept re-visiting the issue, I was still trying to sort through how I felt about it.

I mean, when the truth is the truth, then there's nothing to be upset about, right?

For instance, if someone said I was a cheater or unfaithful in relationships, it wouldn't bother me in the least, because I know for a fact it's not true, and I wouldn't even be upset.

I am an open book and have nothing to hide. I don't get upset when asked questions. In fact, it warms my heart to feel that someone wants to simply get to know me better – to make the effort and attempt to understand me and where I'm coming from – I think that's amazing and always welcomed.

You need to be able to have tough conversations with your partner.

Hearts grow closer after talking through and resolving issues together.

Learning to solve problems together is huge.

LESSON: If your partner gets angry when you ask questions about them, that's a huge red flag. Perhaps consider if that's someone you want in your life if they need to keep secrets from you and lie. Asking questions to learn about your partner is one way to foster emotional intimacy – of which that, coupled with trust, lay the concrete foundation of a healthy, committed, exclusive relationship that will last you a lifetime.

Emotional Abuse

MORE WEEKS HAVE PASSED since the ghosting, but still, I was insistent on maintaining and rebuilding this friendship with her and not "letting a guy come between us." That was my goal.

Not once did I consider = is this friendship even worth it anymore? What was I actually gaining from all this?

It was my conscience. Mainly, I saw a human being in pain who needed a friend during this most painful and challenging time in her life.

I was following the adage, "What would Jesus do?"

Jesus would not want me to let a man who couldn't care less about me get in between a decades-long friendship.

Her and I had history.

I felt an obligation to remain steadfast and continue to be there for her in her time of need.

That's what friends do, right???

However, I was in deep emotional pain, so my ONE request to her – friend-to-friend was simply NOT to talk to me about him.

She said if that's the case that I'm going to be missing out on a lot of important life events with her, because he's that close.

That was a HUGE red flag that this was not going to work.

And, sure enough ... what she do? ...

In the middle of a phone conversation just a few short weeks later, she goes, "He was in town last night!" and proceeded to brag that they both had a wonderful, fun evening together where "He took me to FOUR biker bars to meet all his friends!"

Seriously???

Knife. In. Heart. ... Twisted.

Her bringing him up to me as casually as she did showed me she truly didn't understand (or care about) the brutal emotional, mental, and even spiritual pain he put me through.

I'm not and never will be interested in hearing whatever is going on with him or whatever they are doing together.

Nonetheless, I let it go, and was sincerely happy that she was happy after all she'd been through, since this was shortly after her surgery.

More weeks passed, and all remained well between us.

However, a horrific thing happened to me – that lovely gift he gave me for Mother's Day was run over by a car. It was a freak accident, but I knew right away that it was a sign from God that it was really over between us – without any hope of any sort of future reconciliation or starting over someday, like we both once said we wanted – that it was Divine Guidance telling me the time has come for me to forget about this guy for good.

I was once again utterly and completely devastated. I cried to her about it, and she seemed supportive, which was nice. It looked like we were rebuilding our friendship, as I had hoped would happen, eventually.

Also, during this time, however, I was so desperate for answers, I enlisted the help of a male mutual friend and this is the response I got:

> The response wasn't very detailed … he said he doesn't check messenger much, but was sorry about the gift and thought about getting you a new one but thinks it might be better not to in order to help you get over the relationship. His only comment on that was that you know why it ended and she and I shouldn't be involved in it. He doesn't feel like he needs closure and doesn't want to be mean to you in order to give you closure. I'm sorry I couldn't be more help. Love you girl and hope you find someone you deserve in a relationship.

Well, great that HE doesn't feel he needs closure …

At least he finally realized that SHE shouldn't've been involved, though!

It was now about a month later since the painful phone call I had with her about him coming back to town, now about the last week of August, and so I invited her out to see a regular Thursday night comedy show at a local place with me, intending for us to have some fun together and start to create more positive memories between us.

At the show's intermission, we start to discuss our plans for the upcoming long Labor Day weekend … and, what did she do?? …

She goes, "Oh, I'm making a cheesecake for your friend!"

I'm like, "What friend?"

And she goes, "Him! *(Says his name.)* He's in town through Labor Day and he requested that I make him an Apple Caramel cheesecake for his birthday! So, I gotta work on that this weekend!"

I was in total shock.

AGAIN, she did this.

Seriously???

Knife. In. Heart. … Twisted … Twice over.

This time, I didn't blow up. I didn't freak out. Once again, I let it go and just changed the subject.

That following Monday ... what did she do?? ...

On BOTH Facebook and Instagram, she made a PUBLIC post ... a picture of her gorgeous apple-caramel cheesecake, PINS it at the top of her page, and TAGS him.

He comments, "Thank you, it was beyond delicious!"

Wow.

Just wow.

Knife. In. Heart. ... In Back. ... Across Throat. ... Twisted ... Thrice over.

She just couldn't've had the sensitivity, the consideration, or the decency to block me from that post.

Really??

Mutual friends who knew my pain saw it all and were in shock as well – this person, supposedly my "best friend," doing this to me.

Of course, I had to be the bigger person and be happy for her. Happy for him. Happy for them both.

It's what Jesus would do.

I made the effort to share with her how I felt about all of this, but she dismissed my feelings, criticized me, told me "F#@% you, B!+@#," called me names ("crazy" & "childish"), and said she didn't want to talk about it.

> Oh my God please just let it go I didn't
> need a f#@*g book about it. All you had to
> do was simply say please don't mention his
> name anymore and you did.
> To me this is really childish and you should
> grow up, it's crazy.
> But OK I will never mention his name or
> things I might be doing.
> I will let it go.

(Well, I guess it turns out I DID need a book about it … LOL!)

She then proceeded to tell me that he came by with "a friend," picked up the cake and left – that his visit was only about 15 minutes.

I knew then that what he'd done to me was not something she could ever relate to, and therefore, I needed to limit my interaction with her for my own well-being.

In hindsight, it was at THAT point that I should have cut her out of my life.

I'm just done being abused – emotionally or otherwise – by anyone – I just cannot allow it.

I didn't have the comprehension or vernacular to deal with what was going on in my situation in the most effective way for myself while it was happening back then, but I do now.

And I intend to use it for myself in all relationships from here on out.

I told a mutual friend how I was trying so hard to remain friends with her, but that I just couldn't handle her continuing to shove him in my face.

Here are some words of comfort from my dear friend that I will never forget. This right here is a good friend!

I'm sorry about the thing with her. She should definitely have honored that simple request without getting offended.

To be honest, I'm not a fan of the way she's treating you and I did not really want her to show up.

She should treat him like he never existed in your life not because of him, but for your own healing process. As a friend, she should understand that and if she doesn't, then she isn't the friend you need anymore

My most sincere wish is that she starts to understand how you feel about him and just stop stringing him up in front of you so that you can feel that things can go back to normal

131

Definitely don't settle girl. You are a queen ... or bad b!+@# as my girlfriend would say, LOL!

But how did a "smart, successful woman" get herself in that situation in the first place?

Why do other "smart, successful women" like me get treated this way?

Because we stay.

Because we take them back.

Because we make excuses for them.

Because we justify their behavior.

Because we're too compassionate.

Because we think they will change.

Because we think we can't get any better.

Because we think we'll never feel this way again.

Because we don't want all our time invested to be wasted.

Because we want to save face since they've already met our friends and family.

Because we don't want to give up.

At the end of the day, do you feel loved, cared for and treated well?

If you are disrespected or abused in any way, you need to leave.

As my stories here are showing you, the pain and abuse is often insidious. A modern term for it is called "microaggressions." Sometimes, it's not so prevalent and obvious especially when you have rose-colored glasses on, like me.

I'm living proof you can be positive and compassionate to a fault.

I did not attempt to put up the boundary of her NOT talking about him, until it was too late.

To keep hurting someone repeatedly as described in this book is sheer cruelty and should not be tolerated. To keep allowing yourself to take that kind of emotional abuse from someone is sheer insanity and it needs to stop. It's called "codependency." We think these people are going to change, but they never do.

Nobody's perfect – we all make mistakes, we're only human, we're all God's children, but ...

That doesn't mean you give people license to walk all over you and treat you like dirt.

What this means is to forgive, but place boundaries on how much of your precious, God-given time you spend with people.

You are a gift.

Your time and attention are a gift.

Always remember that.

LESSON: Don't imprison yourself with the idea of "loyalty" or "obligation" where abuse, disregard, and lack of appreciation is happening.

If any part of this lesson resonates with you, please look up motivational speaker Trent Shelton. He has a lot to say about "protecting your peace" regarding folks you have history with – even blood ties to – who are toxic and bring you down.

There IS such an option as loving people and wishing them the best ... from a distance.

When to End the Relationship

I'M A FIRM BELIEVER in talking things out to resolution.

However, it's been my experience that no matter how many discussions I've had, I've been forced to end relationships based on the following three criteria:

The relationship is over when:

- One or both parties refuse to communicate.

- You uncover a non-negotiable difference in core values and ethics.

- One or both parties can't come to a mutual agreement on "the Truth."

God was speaking to me so many times and I just didn't want to listen. As mentioned previously, his gift to me broke in a freak accident. I completely flipped out that night, but fortunately, I was with dear friends who were trying to help me, so I wasn't alone.

One of my friends who was still in touch with him had messaged him on my behalf to try and get him to talk to me for resolution and to let him know I was a mess because his gift to me was now destroyed.

The following is what he replied to my friend, of whom I am forever grateful for sharing with me, so that I could see this with my own eyes.

She knows exactly why there's no "her." She is playing a $#!++* game with you and was with her, too.
I told her when I stopped talking to her why I stopped talking to her. She doesn't want to accept it I guess.
This is what teenagers do when they don't get their way.
I'm not sure what I can say to help you out.
I have no need or want to talk to her.
I'm not being mean to her.
I don't think I should have to act like an angry teenager and call her and say rude and mean things so she'll move on.
I am sorry you have to listen to this cr*p though. I don't know what I can do to help you out my man. You definitely shouldn't have to deal with this.

Yes. I knew.
She asked me a couple of times to just talk to her and I apologized to her because I know I can't just be friendly with Aurora. So there's no way I want to walk in to that nightmare.
Lol and now that I just thought that through … I was thinking I'll buy her another one, but maybe it being run over can help her move on lol

Well – there it was! …

"She is playing a $#!++* game with you and was with her, too."

I FINALLY had my proof that she was talking to him behind my back and that SHE is the one who said something to him to upset him like this!!!

Thank you, God!

But – wow – he says being with me was a "nightmare."

That his time with me was a "nightmare."

It was soul-crushing to read that.

However, nothing was said about the "3 Strikes" game whatsoever that she said he told her he was playing with me.

He says *I* was "playing a game" with HER!

What in the world did she tell him, for crying out loud??

And, really, what does HE know, anyways??

He wasn't even there!

He was never there ONCE when we had our two arguments.

What a fool.

She may be his "best friend," but she is still a woman …

Us women have deep, complex feelings.

She may not have wanted him "that way," but she damn sure wanted to remain his #1.

Like "The Highlander" … "There can be only one."

Only one cook in the kitchen.

One Queen on the throne.

He got played.

Now, I had to think carefully about what to do with this information, because believe it or not – yes, I forgave her again.

Yes, I made up with her again after her public Facebook and Instagram post about her cheesecake gift to him.

I was really trying hard to hang onto this friendship, determined not to "let a guy get in-between us," and to try and continue helping her in her time of need.

So, I let her know I needed to talk to her, that it was important to me …

She refused at first. She said she didn't want to "rehash" everything and wanted to just "let it go and move on."

Thus, I chose to honor her wishes, and not to push her in consideration of her own health issues and loss and everything she's gone through and perhaps was still going through.

However, it was all WAY too painful for me to just "let it go and move on."

Her actions crossed such a boundary with me that "just forgetting about it" wasn't possible.

Every moment of every day and every week and every month that passed that he wasn't speaking to me ...

SHE had a hand in.

The damage she's done to me and the angry feelings she's caused him are something SHE has to live with now.

Finally, she said at the end of our text conversation "We will figure it out" regarding a time and place to talk things through.

In the meantime, I continued to give myself the time, space, and work to heal fully and live my life.

I made a list of questions I wanted to ask her and would show her the above message from him at that time and see if she could please explain to me why he was telling our mutual friend this about me "playing a game" with her, so that I could understand what was going on and find some resolution to this ghosting business he's done to me.

Well, she never got back to me to talk.

She invited me to a charity walk/run with her to be on her team to help raise funds, and I participated with another friend of hers and the three of us had a nice time ...

… but nothing was said about the situation.

I offered to drive her this time for her final surgery (I couldn't last time, because I had my kids), but she said she "already had a ride."

(I told her not to tell me who it was, because I didn't want to know if it was him taking her again, and thankfully, she actually complied this time. So, my guess is that he is the one who drove her again, since she never told me who it was.)

Again, I made another meal for her, as I did for her first surgery, but this time, I dropped it off afterward with a card instead of visiting her.

She texted me thanking me, but still nothing was said about getting together to talk about the situation.

The holidays came and went, and still, no effort was made to talk.

I left the ball in her court because I didn't want to press her and figured we'd talk when the time was right for her.

I was focusing on continuing to live my best life despite what she's done … to forgive, release, and move on.

So, I made plans to go on vacation with good friends out of the country for my upcoming milestone birthday – March 11, 2023.

Ironically, THAT is when she chose to finally mention it. She texted me my 2nd night there, saying she was "sorry for everything."

> Btw ... I'm sorry for everything. Really. I know I've been distant. I had to get my head together. But truly ... have fun. You deserve it. Connect when you get back. :)

Okay.

That was nice, but it wasn't enough, because there were too many things unresolved, unanswered, and so after all these months, since she finally "addressed the elephant in the room" I had my reason to send her the screenshot messages from him above, and here was her response:

> ... that message u shared does not insinuate I had involvement. It states you played a shifty game with me.

Wow.

Really?

Interesting.

141

I was in complete shock.

How can two people look at something and see something entirely different?

Well, this is why there is so much conflict in the world.

Okay, now what?

We're not on the same page about what reality is here.

Not on the same page on what is the truth.

She went on …

> I did not ever say anything to him about you.

> Perhaps he's lying to both of us, did u ever think of that?

> His thoughts are his own

> Hear this … I did not say anything. His feelings about you are because of you

> Not all facts. A lot of what you just said is your perspective

> How he feels about you, what you guys went thru, etc. as with any relationship

> I did stick up for u multiple times, but the only person who can tell you that is him

> Not because I told him … hey, breakup with Aurora

Your list is not accurate

I mean seriously??

And that's where you two need to connect. To clear my name.

I kept asking him what the real issues were and he honestly never told me whole stories and why should he?

And ... for the record I do not lie. Period. I share what I know

Damn I should be proud to think I could motivate people like that ... he is not one to do that. U should know this. XXXX does what he wants because he's XXXX.

I'm not that person I'm sorry u feel that way

I don't lie to anyone, I'd rather tell the truth and hurt them, or not say anything at all.

Here u go. Being mean

Wow.

And about XXXX last year ... yes that however was a lie, we lied to everyone

Have a nice trip.

I proceeded to unleash everything that had been on my mind all these months – and it wasn't pretty.

She was right about that – I WAS being mean, no doubt.

I'm not proud of it.

Also ... what did she have to "stick up for me" about????

I have literally NO idea ...

I particularly lost it when I was telling her that he hates me now because of whatever she said to him, and she lies some more saying she did not "ever" say anything to him about me and he doesn't hate me and "that's all I'll say.":

> He doesn't hate you.

> And that's all I'll say.
> But his thoughts and
> purposes are his own not of
> my doing

Yes, his "thoughts and purposes" are his own, but people draw conclusions based upon the information they get from OTHERS ... from people they TRUST.

He and I were too new.

And, like I said, I never told him all she was saying to me and others, so he didn't know.

And ... right there is a perfect example of this thing she always did by withholding information from me when she said, "... and that's all I'll say." ...

THAT is EXACTLY the shady behavior which triggered me every time with her.

THAT means she COULD say more, because she KNOWS more, but she won't.

Betrayer.

She had a bird's eye view of mine and his relationship from even before its inception, because she knew us both so well, and played us both to a T.

Then, finally ... she said that she'd "listen," and "read my messages," but she's still refusing to tell me the whole truth of whatever she knows ...

Then, finally ... when I said it was important that she listen to what I have to say, she admitted she said something!!!

> Sure. I just can't figure what the life of me what u need to say I haven't heard already. But yes I'll listen. XXXX is XXXX. It should have never happened. And yeah I did mention it.

> Anyway I do hope u have a great time, so nice the trip is on your birthday ...

> Now I have to read your messages ...

At least she FINALLY admitted it ... after almost an ENTIRE year!

"And yeah I did mention it."

She FINALLY admitted she said something to him about our arguments.

On my birthday vacation of course ...

Yet ... she will still REFUSE to be honest and tell me whatever else it is that she knows.

I understood that very moment – that's just who she is ...

I finally accepted that I'd NEVER get the whole truth out of her ...

Only whatever it is that SHE wanted me to know.

From Day One.

And what's funny is that he had the sheer audacity to say that *I* was the one "playing games"!?!?!

Man, if he only knew the truth ... SMDH.

It almost ruined my entire special milestone birthday vacation – and this was only the second night.

But I mean ... when you discover someone had lied to you about one thing, that means they have lied to you before, and they ALWAYS will – that is just a part of that person's nature.

That's just how some people navigate life – using secrets and lies. Not everyone is transparent.

And that's okay ... but just be aware now of who you are dealing with.

I finally saw and realized what kind of person she really was.

I just have to remember that in the future.

So, the following week, I apologized for ending my message to her so harshly, because I sincerely did NOT want to do that, despite having EVERY reason under the sun to feel the way I did.

I told her that I really didn't want my last words to her to be as harsh as they were.

It's just that I was shocked and disappointed by her reaction to what I've shown her.

That I would have had more respect for her had she taken responsibility for her share of the situation that she, I, and he were in ... after seeing his own words proving it.

That I can respect any person who can put their ego aside and say, "I made a mistake, I apologize, and I'm correcting my behavior."

... as I have done with both of them.

I had been patiently waiting all these months for her to keep her word on getting back to me to "figure something out" about hearing what I had to say, because I told her it was important ...

... but she just didn't care because she couldn't figure out what I could have to say"???

Well, that's the point of actually listening to someone to find out.

A true friend says, "Hey, I see you're hurting, I'm hearing that you need to talk, and I'm here for you to listen – and I won't judge you or criticize you, because I respect your feelings."

"And, if I don't agree with what you're saying, I'll still listen, and then explain my point of view with the expectation that you will listen as well, so that we could work this out."

Because that's what actual friends do.

But unfortunately, that was never her attitude.

She chose to do the exact opposite and fan the flame instead.

... as well as choosing to:

... lie to me

... keep secrets and information from me

... and tell me that I'm "being mean" when I am simply communicating to her what I think and feel.

Every single time I tried talking to her about how I felt, it turned into an argument.

... and, then she ran complaining to him about it as well, I came to find.

I've never enlisted anyone to fight my battles for me.

I've always handled my own business myself.

So, I just couldn't understand why she would do that to me, and I just couldn't relate to that kind of behavior.

I'm hurting that I was so wrong about her.

I really thought she had more integrity than this.

I really thought after seeing that screenshot, she'd see I finally had proof that her boy called her out.

She had zero compassion or understanding for the pain I was going through or what I was feeling whatsoever.

It just "pissed her off," when I brought it up, she said.

She belittled me and called me names when I told her how her actions made me feel.

That's just not how a friend treats another friend who is hurting.

And that's also why I felt that everything I've had to say to her was always best written out this way instead of in person or on the phone, so that:

- She could re-read it all later to remember EXACTLY what, and EVERY word I said,

- Nothing is left to "interpretation" or "assumption," so that she shouldn't be twisting anything when she runs and tells him behind my back again, and

- So I don't lose my train of thought or get interrupted.

I mean ... speaking of "being mean" ... what do you call it when a person tells you, "Yeah, sometimes he and I say things just to piss you off or to irritate you ..."

and ...

"I do agree that some of the things I say is mean, but you know what, that is my nature. You do things your way and I'll do things my way."

Wow. Just wow.

All this time, I really wanted to believe that maybe she was just that flaky and didn't mean it, but now seeing her admitting she did it on purpose ... as Maya Angelou said, "When someone shows you who they are – believe them."

Guys come and go, but betrayal is a stain on the soul that will take a mighty long time to clean.

It's too bad she was so focused on "deeply regretting" and being "so sorry" for introducing us ...

... but never "deeply regretting" or being "so sorry" for saying all those rotten, disturbing things to me ...

... nor whispering in his ear about me behind my back to ruin my relationship with him.

If I were her, I'd be "deeply regretful" and "so sorry" for the latter things instead.

How about growing up and taking responsibility for that?

Systematically ruining a relationship between two people.

Two people she supposedly cared about.

Wow.

Simply introducing us was her only act of innocence here!

No one could ever fault her for that.

It's all the disgraceful things she's done afterward that she's got to live with.

I wouldn't wish what she'd done to me with him on ANYONE ... not even her.

I went above and beyond for her for over an entire year and a half of my life, focused on her and everything going on in her life, and been there for her in every way I could, whatever she asked or needed of me.

And I was repaid with insults, slander, and betrayal.

She even accused me of NOT wanting to help her at one point ...!

DESPITE all the times I drove her to her appointments ...

... helped her move (moving furniture, helping pack boxes, helping to pick up floor boards and U-Haul boxes, etc.)

... made meals for her

... gave her cards and gifts

... washed her hair

... spent 12 Thursdays of my life accompanying her to her church group program for a religion I don't even follow (when I could have spent that time finding a man who actually wants to spend his days with me!)

... spent 3 days driving her to and from a hospital in downtown Chicago (tolls and all!)

... drove her to a local hospital to pick up results

... and spent days in hospice with her

... even the very day her relative passed I got her prescriptions from her home and fed and took out her dogs – which, if I hadn't done that she possibly could have missed it!

... ANYTHING she needed and more ...!!!

And I NEVER asked for anything in return.

I never told anyone, nor shoved all this in her face – everything I've done for her ...

... and I never would have mentioned it here, if I hadn't come to learn that she's been telling people I wasn't there for her!

So, I decided to defend myself and tell the world the truth here in this book.

She can lie all she wants, but Lord knows the truth.

I could literally write an entire page on everything I've done for this person.

So, she asked me to help clean her parents' house during the day that Friday for the wake, but I had to work so that was the ONE time I couldn't be there for her.

I felt bad and let her know. Here was our text exchange:

> Because I felt bad I couldn't

> I don't think it's so much that you couldn't I think it's so much more that you didn't want to.

Wow.

Of course, HE was there.

HE busted his behind cleaning that house for her!

... so much so, that he canceled his plans with me that night, claiming to be too tired ...

I mean, that's another thing ... he's done A LOT for her as well ...

... he put in her entire living room floor in her new home

... did work in her new kitchen

... drove 15 hours to be by her side during her first surgery, because I had my kids that weekend ... despite the fact that she had at least SIX other people in her life (that I knew of) who could have done it ...

The pain has been tremendous and indescribable dealing with her.

And exhausting.

So ... as usual, I put my own needs aside ... so badly I wanted resolution with her, and thus, I gave her plenty of time to redeem herself and come to me ready to hear my side.

I gave her a chance to come clean.

Still, I got excuses and denials.

All I ever wanted and needed was to be able to trust her, and for her to show me empathy and compassion (with a generous amount of patience) – things that are to be expected of ANY friend (or, any healthy relationship, for that matter) – but she refused EVERY step of the way ...

... and even gave me solid reasons to doubt her time and time again! ...

... and turned around and insulted me to people to poison their view of me and my character ...

In her response to seeing his message about me "playing a game" with her and her other texts insisting that "it didn't prove anything," she had clearly demonstrated that she was incapable of understanding what she'd done, much less admitting it, nor feeling ANY kind of remorse, empathy, or responsibility.

Also, she wasn't making any sense anymore. She insists she doesn't lie, that she tells the truth all the time, then she admitted one of her lies right there in the same text chain!

She wants to believe that she's an honest person.

"Honest" people tell the truth when asked.

"Transparent" people share information BEFORE they are asked ...

... or caught.

And she's lied in the same text chain EXACTLY like that to me the year before on another issue involving her adult daughter on an issue that she kept from me for 9 months.

NINE months!!

And SHE wasn't even the one to tell me the truth…

I had to dig it out of her daughter ...

... because for some reason, these people just can't seem to be straightforward and direct with me, but instead prefer keeping secrets from me and talking about me behind my back ...

…despite everything I've done for her and her family.

But, alas, that's a whole other awful story ...

I mean …

I was waiting for the day when my "best friend" was truly ready to hear me out to completion with an open heart and mind …

… versus the past passive-aggressive "whatever" or "whatever you say, you're always right!" …

… and eye rolling and head shaking …

… and to honestly and fully answer the many questions I had someday …

… and to actually TELL me things instead of saying, "I wish I could tell you things" that she always loved to say to me …

(Which meant that she was, in fact, keeping things from me …)

… that would have been a productive start to some kind of reconciliation.

But so much time had passed, and that desire never originated from her … she just wanted to sweep it under the rug, like it didn't matter.

I am absolutely clear that this whole thing was always about trust with her – not about "a guy."

She was supposed to be my "best friend" and have my back, but she just didn't.

I can accept that she didn't think something important to me was important to her, and thus didn't mention it – I am a reasonable person, and thus, I can and DO understand that part.

What was unacceptable was the lack of empathy, minimizing my feelings, and never apologizing.

THAT was the issue.

THAT was what I was trying to get from her via our discussions.

THAT never came until that argument which she ended up finally apologizing to me that night ... but then she turned to him and told him about it all, showing that her loyalty lies with him and killing my relationship with him once and for all.

I was always willing to talk and resolve things, but she wasn't.

She refused to even try to understand what I was telling her and what I needed from her.

... and then on top of it, she chose to say mean and disrespectful things on purpose to upset me further and also talk behind my back to people.

This is why I finally ended my relationship with her.

Finally, I had to put up my healthy boundaries and let her go.

I cannot and will not allow someone in my life whom I can't trust.

... someone who pretends to be my "best friend" (my "Bestie"), but then choose to do such things to me.

I now only allow people in my life willing to talk, willing to hear my side, willing to acknowledge that my feelings are valid and important to them out of consideration and respect for me as a person, and willing to do what it takes for the sake of the relationship ...

... people who admit and acknowledge what they did was wrong, and vow never to cross that boundary again, and to honor my boundaries, needs, and feelings.

Period.

That's what a healthy relationship is about.

It's not all one way saying that the other person's feelings and perspective doesn't matter.

Because if that's the case, that others' feelings and perspective doesn't matter, then that's where the relationship ends.

Just like what he did to me.

My feelings and perspective didn't matter to him, and thus he ended the relationship.

My feelings and perspective didn't matter to her, and thus I ended our relationship.

Nonetheless, I had come to understand and accept by now that it was NOT entirely her fault – he is a grown man and could have replied to my messages and reached out to me on his own, but whom obviously is unable to do that.

He blatantly stated that he is literally unable to have a mature, adult conversation …

… that his only option is to "act like an angry teenager" and "call [me] and say rude and mean things" to me.

So, it occurred to me that if the best he could do was "say rude and mean things to me," like a neanderthal, instead of having an intelligent conversation to explain himself, then his silence IS kindness!

He's doing me a favor by just staying the hell away from me, then – exiting himself out of my life.

That epiphany helped me heal.

It's just a shame he had to meet my kids, though. I mean, he knew full well what he was planning, so if I had one clue that he was that kind of person, I NEVER would have introduced him to my kids.

In the days and weeks after, whenever they'd see that gift, they'd tease me … my son said it had "X's and O's" all over it, and my daughter would ask about him.

It was salt in the wound for me days and weeks after …

I simply told them he got a job out of state and that was that which is the truth.

LESSONS:

* Never introduce a partner to your school-age kids until you are in a committed, exclusive relationship.

* Learn to recognize a toxic relationship and end it.

* Learn to make requests. In a relationship (romantic, friendship, business, etc.), if you make a clear request to someone — something important that you need — and they can't or won't respect your request — it's time to end the relationship.

They both should have done that with me — simply ended our relationship, instead of leading me on, being "covert haters," pretending everything was fine, while talking behind my back for months and her continuing to shove her unwavering relationship with him in my face when I specifically asked her not to and then repeatedly denying involvement in his ghosting and refusing to tell me the truth.

It's unbelievable what some people think they can get away with.

And they most certainly will, if you let them.

Apologies

"I'm sorry for everything."

and

"I'm sorry you feel that way."

Classic narcissistic apologies.

There is an article posted September 20, 2020 in "Psychology Today," called "13 Fake Apologies Used by Narcissists," by Dan Neuharth Ph.D., MFT. According to the article, that first "apology" above is called "The One-Size-Fits-All Apology" or "blanket" apology and the second "apology" above is called "The Shift-the-Blame Apology" ("I'm sorry that you …").

Also from the article …

A true apology, by contrast, has most or all of the following characteristics:

- Doesn't contain conditions or minimize what was done.

- Shows that the person apologizing understands and has empathy for the offended person's experience and feelings.

- Shows remorse.

161

- Offers a commitment to avoid repeating the hurtful behavior in the future.

- Offers to make amends or provide restitution where appropriate.

To apologize, one needs to honestly hear what happened from the other person's point of view and how it affected them. But narcissists tend not to be interested in listening to others, particularly if the topic is something the narcissists may have done wrong.

As therapist and author Harriet Lerner wrote, "More than anything, the hurt party needs to know that we really 'get it,' that our empathy and remorse are genuine, that the feelings make sense, that we will carry some of the pain we've caused, and that we will do our best to make sure there's no repeat performance."

Unfortunately, expressing empathy and remorse is often a bridge too far for most narcissists.

Copyright 2020 Dan Neuharth Ph.D., MFT https://www.psychologytoday.com/us/blog/narcissism-demystified/202009/13-fake-apologies-used-narcissists

The "true apology" from her needs to be...

"I am sorry that the entire time you were trying to tell me how you felt that I repeatedly dismissed what you were saying, belittled your feelings, and insulted you."

"I am sorry I took advantage of my friendship and history with him to ruin your guys' relationship and break you up, because I was jealous of the two of you when I actually saw you together."

"I am sorry for continuing to mention him after his ghosting and throw our friendship in your face just to hurt you, after you specifically requested me not to mention him to you anymore, because it was too painful for you."

"I'm sorry that I went around telling people outside the situation bad things about you to defame your character and make them hate you when they knew nothing about the situation.

On my end, I am so incredibly sorry for how I dealt with my own anxiety, insecurities, and past relationship trauma. It wasn't good. I wasn't proud of what my part was in all this.

My "true apology" is within the entirety of this book, as per the bullet listing above:

- I am not seeking conditions or minimizing what I've done.

- I understand and have empathy for their experience and feelings.

- I am incredibly remorseful for my part in it.

- I am committed to avoid repeating my hurtful behavior in the future.

- I tried to make amends, but he refused to talk to me, and she refused to listen when I tried, so there's not much I can do on that last one, unfortunately.

Ironically, I learned an important lesson on apologies from him. It was at his place one evening late March, which I believe may have been the weekend before he left for his new job, and it was just after the conversation we had about giving us a second chance and being exclusive, that we got on the subject of what happened the night we broke up back in October.

I had no idea he was still upset about that! He told me it upset him that I left him for so long and that he wanted me to hang out with his friends, because he specifically invited them there to meet me. I didn't know that, and so I proceeded to say something along the lines that "I'm sorry, but ..." and he said, no, there's no "but."

Now, after reading that article above, I understand exactly what he meant.

I then told him again I was sorry (without the "but") and asked if he believed me. He laughed, shook his head, and said "No!" and I laughed, too, because my instinct told me that he didn't believe me.

So, we discussed it some more and then I once again asked him, "Now, do you believe me?" and he said "Yes."

It was wonderful that we had finally made amends about that night after all this time, which I had no idea still bothered him.

Resolution is a good thing.

LESSON: There is a "right way" and a "wrong way" to apologize. If I ever need to apologize to someone in the future, I will be sure to follow those bullet point characteristics listed in the article above to ensure it is a sincere "True Apology," and that it is complete for a full resolution of the issue to be resolved in peace — once and for all.

Him

IT'S IMPORTANT TO ME to be very careful in this book to not slander or embarrass anyone while honestly and thoroughly sharing my experiences in full, so that's why I'm referring to "he/him" and "she/her," to do that.

That said, I want to explain a bit what the draw was with this guy so that you don't think I'm insane, obsessed, and masochistic wondering why I would spend so much time and energy in pain over this situation from someone who destroyed me emotionally when I should be doing my best to forget about him and bury all evidence. It's because ...

I found him amazing.

In the beginning, he did everything right.

He came on so strong and so fast that I told her he was freaking me out ...

He was on my couch one afternoon asking me about my plans for when my kids graduated high school, because he wanted to move out of state ... that was at the time 7 years into the future!

I hadn't yet thought about what my plans were when my youngest graduates high school, because she was still in elementary school!

He was telling me about his favorite restaurant he wanted to take me to (which, I never visited yet to this day), and about a road trip he wanted to take me on (which, I would have LOVED to have gone on!), and people he wanted me to meet ... I loved EVERY moment of being a part of his future plans and I was looking forward to all of it!

He painted a beautiful picture for us.

I was SO on board ...

Secretly.

Because I was too scared to tell him.

Maybe my intuition was telling me something ...

He was Leo, the Lion, and he embodied every bit of it.

Poor guy, I fought him the whole time in the beginning.

I was so focused on Eros, who I thought was a perfect match for me, but broke my heart completely at the time.

I remember the day I told Eros that I was giving this new guy "Him" a chance.

He was hurt, but he understood.

I felt a true connection with this guy, even deeper than Eros, and I will tell you why ...

You're going to love this one ...

Speaking of "Narcissists," alright ...

He reminded me of myself.

There, I said it.

I know that sounds utterly and disgustingly narcissistic, but it's true.

He was probably the only man I've ever dated in my life who I would define as truly "strong."

Almost as strong as I am.

He seemed to embody my personal motto, "The Will to be Victorious."

I even looked up the meaning of his name, just for kicks, and apparently, it means 'high, noble,' and could also mean 'strength'.

Of course.

He's been through a lot, owned up to his mistakes, and was taking significant, honorable action in his life to have it end up better than it's been thus far.

Shortly before he met me, something in his mind decided that he wanted more from himself; that he wanted a better life.

Then, he found and pursued me – simply from our mutual friend's Facebook page is the story that she told me. (Even though HE said she'd been telling him about me for "all this time" – so much so that he thought I was two different people, he said!)

He found it pleasantly amusing that, "We were from two different worlds" he once said in my living room.

I gave him a glimpse of mine and what was possible for him – a different level than he's ever experienced before.

He invited me into his, too, and I was excited to try new things that he was eager to show me.

We had so much to look forward to.

I was excited that he was focused on his future, not his past.

Just like me!

I loved that.

I also loved that he enjoyed the same activities I liked = volleyball, bowling, and pool. We never got to bowl together, though, nor play pool against each other.

I loved that he could dance, too. We never got to slow dance or "club" dance together, but we danced polka-type at an Oktoberfest celebration, which was fun! It reminded me of when I'd dance polka with my family at my grandparents' house growing up.

I loved that he was willing to dress up with me for Halloween, too. I've only done that once – with my ex-boyfriend in my 20's for a Halloween party. That's it. My ex-husband wasn't into it. I was always the one who liked to dress up with our kids and go trick-or-treating with them.

We also enjoyed trying my "Beer Club of the Month" beers each month from a local brewery I supported.

We even preferred to shop at the same grocery store chain.

And our vacation ... ugh ... we were both SO looking forward to that vacation that never happened. What an amazing experience that would have been! Planning for that was a huge step in our relationship, and SO exciting for us!

But, as my feelings grew, so did my fear, and I held back.

Oddly enough, we were both surprised to discover that we'd already met 16 years prior at our mutual friend's wedding. He had a girlfriend then, and I was married – this was way before I even had my kids. I even found a picture I'm in with his then-girlfriend! How strange!

The more I got to know him, the more aspects about him were coincidental and just "fit" – it was astonishing.

Because of our friendship with her, we were only ONE degree away from each other our entire adult lives, and never knew it.

I found out even in high school, he wasn't far from me growing up, so we discovered we even hung out at the same place, and he most likely knew people I knew as well. Again, we could have bumped into each other during those years at some point and not even known it.

Meeting him was inevitable.

... it just had to be the right time.

That said, it was Divine Timing that we didn't meet a moment sooner than we did, because it would have been a "hard no" for me, LOL!

It was serendipitous.

I admire people who come out from a bad place and turn themselves around. It impresses me. Not everyone can do it. It's not easy. Self-motivation, tenacity, drive ... these are all things you either have or you don't. You can't beg, borrow, or steal that kind of fire.

I know for a fact that he can accomplish anything he sets his mind to, because he's got that fire inside of him.

In the short time I've known him, it seemed he'd never settle for less.

He wanted quality.

He had a vision and a plan for himself.

He seemed to me to be a man who knows what he wants ... and goes for it.

So, I admired that about him, too. Some people are lazy about their visions, then wonder why they never get anywhere. If you have no path, then how will you ever reach your destination?

My mother said I've always had that fire, too – that I was born with it. She'd laugh because when I was a child, I used to see things on commercials or in catalogs and say, "I WANT it!" It's true.

And anything I wanted, I worked hard to get. Nothing was handed to me. I didn't come from money, power, or prestige. My family were all manual laborers.

My Sicilian grandmother worked in a factory with her family at a very young age, and my Polish grandfather was a truck driver. My father was a delivery driver, and my uncle was a mechanic-turned-delivery driver.

I know what it means to earn something and to make something happen out of nothing.

That's where he would have fit in perfectly with my uncle and grandparents, had they still been alive, and my dad. It's the family I was raised in.

This guy had lots of "dealbreakers" for me, though. Had I seen him on a dating app, I would have swiped left in a heartbeat.

So, when we met through our mutual friend ("her"), as I said, I fought it at first, despite my initial attraction.

Since I was getting over Eros, I was not interested in this guy's "dealbreaker" aspects, even though I did feel that "spark" right away and I told her so after our first meeting.

Then, week after week, he won me over.

It happened naturally and gradually, as it should.

I didn't want our team to know yet for one reason and one reason only = he never asked me.

He didn't yet ask me to be his woman.

I wanted HIM to ask ME.

I felt he didn't deserve the benefit of everyone thinking we were a couple if we weren't.

One evening, he invited his other best friend (a male) there to play and I guess meet me. She was there too. I found it so odd that apparently, this guy didn't know who she was … I mean, if he and she were "best friends," then how did this other best friend of his NOT know who she was?? I found that odd …

Anyway, this guy seemed upset that I wanted to keep it under wraps at the time that he and I were seeing each other, as if I was ashamed of it, and that was definitely NOT the case whatsoever. This is the reason = simply because he didn't ask me yet … and I really wanted him to.

It was just like that scene in "Back to the Future" Part 1 where George McFly was dancing with Lorraine and she asked him, "George, aren't you going to kiss me?" and he was hemming and hawing … like that, except I didn't ask him to ask me or ever bring it up until one Saturday months later in September … I was hoping he'd just read my mind, LOL!

After we made it "Facebook Official," however, anyone and everyone in our presence knew. We are both very physically affectionate people.

My "Love Language" is basically tied between "Words of Affirmation" and "Physical Touch." I'm a hugger, in general, and definitely more with my partner. (i.e., holding hands, arms around each other, kisses, stroking hair, sitting on his lap, etc. ...)

I have no doubt if I had him take the test that his "Love Language" is "Physical Touch," then probably "Quality Time."

I kept this text because it touched my heart so deeply:

> You are a strong, beautiful, smart woman. Not used to all 3 in 1 woman LOL

Plus, he used to say something to me no other man ever had that really touched my heart ... on more than one occasion, he'd say, "I like the way you think."

That told me he felt I was more than just a pretty face.

> I like the way you think. Let me see what time we get done and how long it takes to get home but yes. I like that idea

I liked it when he said that, because most of his compliments seemed to be always about how I looked to the point that I was beginning to think there was nothing else about me he liked.

Once again, he touched my heart very deeply one day when he said, "Do you even know how beautiful you are? Do you have any clue?"

These messages were my favorites, though:

> Good night beautiful

> Good morning most beautiful girlfriend. How's my hotness today?

> Hotness! I was literally gonna text you "Hotness" this morning …
>
> OMG. This is getting scary … LOL!

These next two text exchanges I wish I would have paid more attention to. These were the most important ones …

> … it was out of my control. Wasted many good years of my life.

I understand that. I'm happy to try as well but previous dating history makes me cautious. That being said, I really have enjoyed all my time with you so far, so I'm willing to give it my all.

I can say ... I'm really surprised and mostly happy this has happened. I really enjoy our time. Not just our alone time, but the sport hasn't changed since day 1. It's all time I'm enjoying.

That's great to hear!

I can honestly say that the time I've been spending with you I enjoy as well so far!

Mostly is a bad choice of words actually. I'm more so ... happy.

It's a sad irony that he didn't give me his best compliment until our last videochat when he said I was a "smart, successful woman."

I would have loved to hear more of his feelings about me in that regard – like about my character or other aspects about me – besides my looks – even though I loved it when he said that, too, like how I was "all 3 in 1 woman."

But he was so different! I laughed to God, "You're really funny, God! This is a good one you pulled on me."

I mean – he wasn't even my "type," physically …

As you read in my early post-divorce relationships, I went for guys at LEAST 6' …

Tall, big, fit, athletic …

Makes me feel safe and protected.

He was fit because of his job, but not tall or "big," just average height.

This guy was literally the polar opposite of Eros. Even Eros' LinkedIn profile picture was like an Angel (wearing a professional suit with a light blue background) and his was like the Devil (literally with painted "Devil wings," which we had matching profile pictures taken at a place called "Afterlife," that had "Devil" and "Angel" wings on the wall to pose against).

He kept the picture I took of him as his profile picture ever since (as far as I know), for over two years as of this writing. I remember that night very well. We saw a Queen cover band from Canada. She and I took pictures of ourselves with both the "Devil" and "Angel" wings, but he was sitting up by the bar, so I went and showed him and I knew that he needed to take the one with the "Devil" wings, so we walked down there and I positioned him and his arms against those wings perfectly when I took the picture and sent it to him.

A day or so later, when I showed my other friend both these men's profile pictures, we had a good laugh about the difference!

Some friends to this DAY who have never met him have NO idea how I could have been attracted to him, given he was missing teeth and had weathered skin, among our other significant peripheral differences, and they'd insist that I could do SO much "better" …

But I knew … "Different, but same," like that line Mr. Miyagi told Daniel in "The Karate Kid" about Daniel and Ali.

And … I understood and accepted his issues because obviously, I have issues too.

Our energies were compatible.

Our mutual male friend said that he "really liked us together."

That was an astute observation, and I'm so grateful he noticed and shared that with me.

I knew what he meant.

I felt it, too.

His comment meant a lot, because he's known me in high school and then has gotten to know my adult character and personality … as well as gotten to know HIS character and personality … and then seeing in person how the two of us interacted with each other on a weekly basis.

We had chemistry and made a great team.

Many times, you see two people together and think how different they are, why would they be together at all? … until you interact with them and get to know them.

Like the Paula Abdul song, "Opposites Attract." That's true that sometimes it may seem that way … but when you take away those external nuances, what's inside? You'll be surprised to find a match.

The heart wants what the heart wants, and it is illogical.

It's unexplainable and divine.

I hung on to the one memory I had of him that made it significantly difficult for me to reconcile in my mind what he'd done to me …

That conversation we had in March, just before he left for his job in April, when I asked him point blank if I should let him go, and he said …

… "I would love to tell you no."

In my mind, that told me he didn't want me to let him go.

So, I didn't.

I hung on and he never left my thoughts, despite his schedule, willing to remain steadfast and see what it was like, even though he didn't want me to.

When he came back that Mother's Day weekend and gave me that gift, he told me the schedule was such that he is told where he's working next sometimes only a day or two in advance, so that he can't even make plans with his own family, and that I would hate it.

True that would drive me crazy, because I'm a planner – especially because I only have my kids half the time, so I always plan my personal life around the days I don't have them.

But he never once asked me if that was something I'd be willing to try …

I mean, in terms of physical touch, I'm the type of woman who'd rather wait a month or so for a steak dinner than get a "Happy Meal" every week.

Plus, we've already proven we're quite proficient in video chatting.

He never knew that if given the choice, I'd rather spend an evening video chatting with him than going out.

He never knew I looked into where other job opportunities for myself may be in the states he was interested in moving to actually consider that possibility when my kiddos DO move out someday.

I was going to surprise him.

Sadly, he was strong, but not wise.

Between that decision, and how blindly he was swayed by what he was hearing – he truly disappointed me in the end.

He told me in the beginning that he was a person who researched issues to "find out both sides" and "make an informed decision."

Clearly, he didn't do that with me.

My insecurities conclude that I just wasn't worth it to him, and that he used his job as an excuse to get rid of me once and for all, so he could get his needs met on the road free and clear rather than be a cheater like he said his ex was.

All this said, I am well aware that I'm only operating on the memory of him, the good times, the plans we had, and most importantly, how he told me that he didn't want me to let him go.

So, everything I wrote about him in this chapter – the man I thought he was ... I fully realize now that may not be accurate.

It's entirely possible I gave him and our relationship "excess meaning" ... that I made him more important than he was, and that I assumed he had other good qualities that he really didn't, just because he had one or two good qualities – I learned this is called the "Halo Effect."

Therefore, I'm making it a point to remember that he wasn't ALL that great ... there were some concerning issues ...

Number one for me was that he was pretty set on wanting to move out of state. I was so scared I'd end up really falling for him and having him meet my kids and two years later when his lease was up, he'd move – my abandonment issues were triggered already.

But when I told her, she said "Oh, it's just him! Do you really think he's going to move?" I said, "How should I know, he's YOUR friend!" She didn't seem to take him seriously at all, but I was definitely concerned.

Second, I remember one night I was driving us in the rain and he raised his voice to me because of the harsh way I was stopping and going over bumps – he said his back was hurting him, and I told him something to the extent that was just the way it is, and what I meant was that my brakes are very touchy – he thought I was doing it on purpose. Right away, he said, "I'm sorry, you didn't deserve that." He was right, of course, I didn't deserve that, and so I accepted his apology, but kept it in the back of my mind that had better not happen again.

Third, he used to ruin our dates with his angry political rants. He was so upset about things. I understood his position, and I listened as well as I could, but he just wouldn't stop. A couple of times, he literally almost made me cry, because we just weren't having fun anymore, and that wasn't how I expected our evening to go. It was getting to be a pattern I wasn't happy with. But did I tell him? No. I told her.

Even at one of our most fun, romantic dates, he started in again on the politics and I lost it and almost started crying again, but instead I screamed at him for not getting the vaccine and I took off for the ladies' room to cool down. Not proud of that moment! I came back to the table, apologized, and we made up and had a great rest of the evening. In fact, I'm almost positive it was that night after the event that we decided to make it "Facebook Official" and change our relationship status, LOL! Weirdos …!

Fourth, I noticed he liked to talk about himself a lot – his past, his goals, his job – but didn't seem too interested in me or what made me tick – my past, my goals, my job. In fact, I don't recall him asking me very many questions about myself at all. I remember some nights trying to get a word in edgewise, but he was on a roll, and I could not. Perhaps it could be because I was an open book as it was, or maybe because anything he wanted to know he got the information from her. I'll never know.

At the end of the day, it seems as though either he just wasn't emotionally mature enough for a healthy lifelong romantic relationship, or he just didn't care about me anymore … or both … and I didn't know it until it was too late.

At this point, I'm well aware that the pain I feel from this ordeal is only this:

- the memory of the good times

- my imagination of what I thought we were aiming towards

- the humiliation of being so utterly wrong about him

- the betrayal of someone I thought was my "best friend."

That's all it comes down to.

I mean, clearly, I'm not missing out on him as a person, because he's not a good man to have done this to me.

I know I deserve better.

The dual feelings of betrayal (her) and degradation (him) in this experience are what hurts.

Or, perhaps, it just wasn't the right time for us to have a lasting thriving relationship, due to the many serious and complicated factors beyond our control, as I've explained in this book.

Our lives aligned for that short amount of time, and affected me so deeply, it's something I will never forget.

And, because this experience was so impactful to me personally on many levels, I had to immortalize it to capture these important lessons for myself, so as never to forget and end up making the same mistakes in the future.

In a sense, I wonder if this isn't my karma for not taking seriously my boyfriend in my 20's whom I was with for 6 years, because I didn't consider him to be "husband material" …

He lived with his parents, was a mechanic by trade (although he had a car he couldn't fix) smoked, played video games all day, and wasn't interested in doing much more than that in life … although we never fought – ever. We got along very well, and he respected me – he called me his "better half" to all his friends. He was very kind.

I just had different thinking back then.

Coincidentally, he turned out to be a sci-fi writer!

LESSON: Don't automatically count out a potential partner because you believe them to be "too different." If someone is into you and you feel any kind of "spark," it's important to pay attention to that.

Get to know someone on the inside – how they think, what their character is like, what their plans are, and what motivates them. You may be pleasantly surprised.

Have Faith that God knows what God is doing.

Grief

BY FAR, WHAT HE's done to me with this ghosting is the cruelest thing anyone has ever done to me in my entire life.

… to date, at least.

… except, of course, what she did to me with her months of betrayal.

Someday when my kids read this, I hope they learn to never "ghost" someone – to give people simple human dignity to respond to messages and to always try and resolve things and have closure on both sides whenever possible.

To be straightforward and transparent with people instead of shady and dishonest.

To never do to someone what these people did to me.

It is utterly degrading and completely traumatizing, with lingering pain and despair.

I lost both a "best friend" and romantic relationship with someone I really cared about.

I lamented to a dear friend that it's like he died.

She wisely suggested I seek grief counseling.

I thought that was brilliant, and it so happened that my church was offering their annual group grief workshop for 8 weeks, so I immediately signed up.

It turned out to be an important part of my healing journey and I am forever grateful my friend thought to suggest it to me.

It was a terrible, ironic thing that my long-time counselor just so happened to have retired a month before the ghosting, so I've been self-counseling all this time (it was now late October 2022).

Therefore, after the new year when my insurance benefits started up again in January with some free sessions, I decided to seek a new counselor. This time, instead of one specializing in anxiety, I found one specializing in grief. I worked with this grief counselor for about 6 months solely on this issue, and she was a tremendous help in my healing as well.

The 5 stages of grief and loss from Elisabeth Kubler-Ross are the following:

1. Denial and isolation
2. Anger
3. Bargaining
4. Depression
5. Acceptance

Elisabeth Kubler-Ross was a Swiss psychiatrist who wrote a book called "On Death and Dying" in 1969 after working with terminally ill patients at the University of Chicago.

She claimed later in life that these stages are not linear or predictable, but instead, a person can experience them in a random order, if at all.

I've experienced each and every one of these in full and in repeated linear and non-linear cycles in both this situation and during my divorce, and am happy to say, I've finally reached "Acceptance."

LESSON: A breakup or divorce is a valid reason to mourn and get help for grieving. Please care for yourself in this way if and when you need to.

Advice

IN THE MONTHS AFTER the ghosting, I dove into deep self-work and fighting against the grief best I could to heal. I was blessed to have two close "far-removed-from-the-situation" friends who were with me every step of the way. They really did their best to support me and for that, I am forever grateful.

One of them has some psychic ability and was convinced he'd contact me in a specific month that was about six months away. That was quite a long time, so I wasn't "holding my breath," but I was so much in pain that I chose to hold onto hope for that day.

When that month came along, I hadn't heard from him yet, so she advised me to call this other psychic who was a "real" one and said that he could help me.

In desperation to try anything to help myself get answers and resolution, I called.

Wow – was this guy good!!! All I gave him was a first name and date of birth and he told me things he could NOT have possibly known in doing an internet search.

So, I had real hope at this point.

Unfortunately, the month came and went, so I called him again, and this guy gave me another month or two deadline ...

Then, that deadline came and went.

Oddly enough in the meantime, his face kept coming up in my Facebook Messenger every time I composed a message to someone.

He and I hadn't been connected on social media for months, so I had no idea why this was happening.

I searched up how to remove it and tried everything short of blocking, because I really don't believe in that, and I didn't want to do it.

It was breaking my heart over and over every time I'd see his face, though, every single time I composed a message from my phone. He was the first one showing up on my list and I didn't understand why.

I wasn't checking his page, because for one, I was too scared to see him most likely back with his ex (for convenience, even though he said he hated her) or another woman just yet, and also, he never posted anything public, so since we weren't Facebook friends, I wouldn't've seen anything anyway.

So, I just let it go, but now it was nearing a year into the ghosting, and I ended my friendship with the person who sabotaged us as gracefully as I could muster, making sure to forgive her, and so I thought perhaps I could at least reach out in a kind way to this guy in order to have a peaceful goodbye as well.

Therefore, I contacted the psychic for a final reading, and he told me to reach out, and so I did, against my better judgment – I figured I had nothing to lose.

I sent him a video instead of a message, so he could see I had no hard feelings, and just kept it friendly and light and let him know what was going on with our team, and that's all.

He read it, but no reply.

Okay, well, I was happy that I tried, but at this point, I had to block him, and I didn't want to, but I let him know I had to and so I said a nice friendly goodbye as much as I could.

About a month or so later, it was now around the anniversary of the ghosting, and I figured I'd try one last time for a peaceful resolution – thinking that perhaps maybe enough time went by, and he'd be finally willing to simply explain what happened.

I unblocked him and sent a huge message.

He read it but didn't reply.

I was humiliated and devastated once again, and tried to block him again, but Facebook wouldn't let me re-block him until 48 hours.

So, I figured I'd use this opportunity to my advantage and let him know anything and everything I wanted to say to him to get it all off my chest … and so I did.

It was a similar practice to when you go to the grave of a dead person and just start talking to them – like that.

It felt great to say whatever I wanted, uninterrupted!

He just kept reading, but not replying.

That's some real hate for someone right there!

... To literally see that they are in pain, messaging you heartfelt communications ...

... and you stone-cold ignore it.

... over and over and over again.

... without reacting or replying at all.

I've never known such utter cruelty in my life, aside from discovering what she'd done to me by constantly badmouthing me to him and playing a game with him against me to say things to upset me.

It was so utterly strange to me as to why he didn't just tell me off. Why didn't he just tell me that he hated me, that didn't want anything to do with me, and to stop reaching out?

So, I told him that at this point, HE was going to have to block me, since obviously I have no self-control here.

He honored my request and blocked me.

I'm really glad he did. I would have written him this entire book, I bet! I've already written him enough to have been a book for sure.

It was good he blocked me for a few reasons …

For one, I didn't want it on MY Karma.

For two, now he can't see any of my public posts, because I post a lot publicly – funny memes on my page and heartfelt memes on my story.

For three, now his face was finally gone and doesn't show up when I create a message!

Whew! Thank God!

I also deleted the entire conversation on my Messenger, too, so that it's completely gone, and I can't see his face there either, because it was still showing, even though he blocked me. Facebook Messenger is strange like that.

Back when he first ghosted me, I searched and erased all our posts, so that they wouldn't come up on "Facebook Memories," and that was one of the smartest things I did, because now it's all gone, so I don't have any system reminders.

I'm finally protected on social media!

But did you see what I did there for all those months? For a long while there, I completely and utterly gave my power away to others about what I should do instead of empowering myself and trusting myself on what I should do.

I was looking for someone to validate what I wanted to hear instead of the truth.

In hindsight, I see that what these people were telling me, they were really telling themselves – if they were in my shoes. Just like I'm doing here. Their advice is their "lessons learned."

I appreciated that, and was very grateful, but I forgot that ultimately, I am my own Guru.

Now, I could argue that doing any or all of the things I wish I would have done doesn't mean that he would still be here today … but, at least I wouldn't live with the regret of what could have been, because *I* was the one holding myself back by not listening to my own guidance.

LESSONS:

* Do NOT give your decision-making power in your relationship over to anyone else.

You are ultimately your own authority. YOU are your own "Guru." You know what you should do. Our conflict arises when we don't WANT to do what we KNOW we must do. Sometimes, we must make hard decisions and take action that is best for us.

* Make decisions based on the facts you have on hand – not imaginary possibilities that you have no basis to believe.

Karma

Fun fact about me ... I'm as fearful of protecting my Karma as some folks are afraid of the Devil.

I've seen it happen throughout my life, right before my eyes, so I don't mess around with that – not in any of my relationships. It's a priority for me to make sure that no matter what, my Karma is clean with everyone to the best of my ability.

This is why I'm so big on resolution – doing whatever it takes to talk issues through and to sincerely apologize when I've made a mistake.

I value my relationships with others. I don't "ghost" or give up easily. Even in my marriage – I went through three marriage counselors, and filed a first time, but didn't go through with it, then only filed the second/final time when he literally told me to just go ahead and divorce him rather than comply with a request I had made.

Him telling me to do it was the only way I could possibly "give up" on my marriage and put my kids in this inconvenient dual-home situation, because I really didn't want to. I fight for the things that are important to me.

My earliest experience with Karma that I can recall was when I was probably in 6th grade or so, walking down the main street of my town. There was this kid who used to say mean things to me, and he was riding his bike and passed me up from behind and called me "Gruesome."

Well, a few minutes later, he was riding back, facing me this time and when I saw him coming, I shouted "Gruesome!" to him back, but I didn't notice until he got closer … it looked like he'd been in a fight … his face was red, his lip was bleeding and looked like he had a black eye and tears down his face.

I felt SO horrible!!!

Unfortunately, apparently, he got his.

Later in life, between my Junior and Senior year of high school, I had a confrontation with a girlfriend of an ex-boyfriend who had physically harmed me in our relationship, and he gave her a glass "Snapple" jar that she busted across the side of my forehead. I still have the scar to this day, as well as one on my chin when he pushed me so hard that my chin put a hole in his parents' hallway wall.

A few years after that, someone told me that he was pushed through a glass window in a confrontation at a party and died. It's true that he passed away, but I am not sure of that story. Nevertheless, it really freaked me out.

Glass.

Very strange.

This is why I pray, and I do NOT wish folks harm. No one. No matter what they've done to me, I do not wish them harm. It's important to pray for peace.

I know that I can hold my head high knowing I would never be so low as to sabotage someone's relationship behind their back like she did or ignore someone's repeated attempts to reach out to me like he did.

I make better choices than that to protect my Karma.

I have no regrets in my last correspondence to them.

Unfortunately for her, unless and until she fixes what she's done to us (which is impossible at this point), she's got that on her head for the rest of her days.

She's got to live with what she's done.

LESSON: Do NOT mess with Karma. Be cognizant of your actions and do your best to make amends with people to the best of your ability. If you need to end a relationship, send them off in peace and do NOT do or say things to purposely hurt them or wish them harm in any way. Everything shakes out in the end, one way or another. "Protect your peace." ~ Trent Shelton

Mental Health

I WAS DIAGNOSED WITH Generalized Anxiety Disorder (GAD) in the late '90's. I remember my first panic attack was on the expressway on my way home from work. I was changing lanes and turned to look over my shoulder and all of a sudden, my heart started racing and I couldn't slow it down. I really thought I was having a heart attack.

When I got off the expressway onto the road, I called 911 on myself and took my first ambulance ride. I got to the hospital, they checked me out, and everything was fine. Diagnosis = panic attack. I contacted a psychiatrist via my insurance and, although I was holistic-minded, I agreed to a 6-month prescription of Xanax along with sessions to get a handle on it. It worked until I started getting them again after I had my kids.

Fortunately, I was able to get it under control once again (without medication this time), but I started to get them again when things were going bad with my marriage before I filed for divorce the first time. After I filed the second time and was finally divorced, I moved into my current home in 2019 and haven't had one since, as of this writing.

Most of the time, I have my anxiety under control. I do the things I'm supposed to do to manage it, such as keep active, exercise, eat healthy, journal, and focus on the good and positive things in my life.

However, when I have an issue, it's sometimes hard for me to figure out how to resolve it quickly – I take a lot of time processing it. I'm a thinker and an extremely sensitive person. I am not one that just says, "Okay, I'm fine now, moving on!" in a heartbeat like that. I feel things deeply, and for a very long time. It takes quite a while for me to heal from emotional trauma.

It takes exceptionally compassionate people around me to understand that.

Through my journey working through my own issues since the ghosting, I discovered that (obviously!), I have the "Anxious Attachment" relationship style, and that I was also Codependent, on top of it. Here is what Psychology Today describes it as:

> Codependency is a dysfunctional relationship dynamic where one person assumes the role of "the giver," sacrificing their own needs and well-being for the sake of the other, "the taker." The bond in question doesn't have to be romantic; it can occur just as easily between parent and child, friends, and family members.

Upon reflection, I feel I've done that in my marriage and certain friendships, for sure, such as the one described in this book, which is exactly why I included it.

In fact, it's been my experience to learn in both my in-person and online groups that most sensitive, "aware/

conscious," and spiritual people seem to do this to ourselves.

Here are the symptoms of "Anxious Attachment" style, which described me to a "T", that I'll need to work on:

- Signs of codependency
- Intense emotional discomfort or avoidance of being alone
- Difficulty setting boundaries
- Fear of abandonment
- Feeling like you're unworthy of love
- Feeling dependent on others
- Frequent need for validation
- An intense desire for intimacy or closeness
- Tendency to feel or act jealous
- People-pleasing tendencies
- Low self-esteem
- Sensitivity to changes in how others feel, speak, or behave
- Tolerating unhealthy behaviors in relationships
- Difficulty trusting others

https://psychcentral.com/health/anxious-attachment-style-signs#signs-of-anxious-attachment-style

Mental health is a very important subject and is something that should be taken seriously when you're in a relationship. I know what it's like to be involved with someone with depression as well – it's no joke.

I believe a lot of people have some kind of mental health issue to some degree, and it should NOT be shamed. It is very common, and if diagnosed, can be handled. It doesn't have to be a dealbreaker if the person is willing to get help.

In fact, that's the one thing I will NOT apologize for … my mental health issues = anxiety, "Anxious Attachment" style, and insecurities. My anxiety is inherited. I own it. I'm aware and working on it. I'm human. I'm doing my best. That's all I can do.

Next time I'm in a committed relationship, however, I now know to disclose that upfront, so it's out in the open.

If anyone wants to get angry or irritated with me for that, then they are simply not for me, and can please move along. The right man will understand and be compassionate and patient with me, because he'll feel I'm worth it.

One morning, I happened to catch this verse of a song on the radio:

Well good for you
You look happy and healthy, not me
If you ever cared to ask
Good for you
You're doing great out there without me, baby
Like a damn sociopath

This is from the song "good 4 u" by Olivia Rodrigo, and so I decided to look up the lyrics of the entire song, because that verse resonated with me so much. Sure enough, it seemed there were certainly parts of that song I could have written about my situation, to an extent (not all).

Thus, I decided to look up exactly what the definition of a "sociopath" was, and found this description in a Healthline article:

> "Sociopath" is an informal term that's often used to refer to someone who has antisocial personality disorder (ASPD). ASPD is a personality disorder that involves a lack of empathy in addition to manipulative behaviors and impulsiveness in some people.
>
> https://www.healthline.com/health/sociopath-signs#signs-in-adults

The number one aspect of this condition is listed as lack of empathy. It says, "… they may simply not care that their actions hurt someone."

Other aspects are:

- Disregard for right and wrong
- Wit and charm
- Impulsiveness
- Arrogance
- Aggression

Wow – I was really onto something here! This could possibly finally explain how he was able to "ghost" me like he did, and repeatedly disregard my attempts at reaching out.

And it could also explain how she could purposely continue to mention him to me when I specifically asked her not to and make that public post on social media.

I looked up another article or two to get more information and they all mention this condition is similar to that of a "psychopath." So, I researched the definition of that, too, and discovered that one of the first aspects of psychopathy listed is also "lack of empathy and remorse."

Both of these conditions list "lack of empathy" as the primary symptom, which is possibly how he could have the ability to keep reading my messages, but not reply or "react" to any of them, and never apologize.

Or – had he just completely shut down emotionally after he ghosted me?

If so, why?

At least now, I have another piece of the puzzle to try and make sense of this situation for my own closure and resolution.

I had been too trusting of a person, but now, I am more cautious since learning about all of these mental health issues – not to mention the all-important narcissism and alcoholism – in order to be more careful of who I date in the future – not only for my own safety and wellbeing, but also, because I am a mother of two school-age children at the time of this writing.

Knowledge is certainly power!

LESSON: Learn about these mental health conditions I listed: Anxiety, Codependency, Alcoholism, Narcissism, and Antisocial Personality Disorder (to identify a possible Sociopath or Psychopath you may be dating).

Abandonment Issues

So, as I mentioned earlier, I discovered I had serious abandonment issues.

I'm happy to say they didn't come from my Dad, because he was always there for me growing up, every day, like clockwork. I have no issue there.

I was in my 20's when I got into the study of all things "New Age," and learned of the concept of reincarnation and past lives that I remembered one of my past lives, which explains everything.

I believe I was a Native American of some kind of prestige in our tribe, and my husband was a warrior. We had two very young children. They may have been both girls. He was called to war, and I didn't want him to go. I was very angry that he said he had to, and so he went. He was killed. I never got over it.

This also explains my affinity for the Native American culture. I have a set of "Soulmate" plates of a Native American couple that mean a lot to me.

I have not responded well to losing the men in my life.

I was very close to my Uncle Louie. He was like a mix between my older brother and my second Dad. He always got me the coolest gifts, taught me how to shoot pool, and took me on my first motorcycle ride.

When he got married to my lovely Aunt Linda when I was about 15, I acted horribly at their wedding. I was crying like he was dying. For some inexplicable reason, I felt I'd never see him again. It was awful, and I'm terribly ashamed of my behavior. My aunt is a wonderful person and of course later in life I apologized to her, and I do my best to keep in touch, because as tragedy would have it, my uncle actually did end up passing away suddenly at the age of 48 while working.

Our family was absolutely devastated, and I was a mess.

I recall 10 years earlier, the day my grandfather (his father) had also passed away.

Shortly after that, my boyfriend of 6 years broke up with me after being one of my grandfather's pallbearers, and I was an absolute wreck.

Looking back, something in my heart closed at that time.

I didn't know what unconditional love was until my William was born, then my Victoria. I named him "William" because I believed he was God's Will. I was going to name Victoria "Elizabeth Grace," but a few months into the pregnancy, she told me her name was "Victoria," and so she is "Victoria Elizabeth," named after two Queens, because she is "victorious."

That is why my axiom is "The Will to Be Victorious."

I believe I was born with this, and why I am so attracted to and inspired by people who also have this inherent gift.

With this ghosting, what he had done to me needed to be done for my soul's growth so that I could heal my abandonment issues in this lifetime.

Because I was unhealed, when I was faced with someone in my life that I had such strong feelings for, I tried to fight it best I could and failed.

I was so scared because of these abandonment issues. So, I self-sabotaged, and I didn't even realize it until it was too late.

The irony is not lost on me here that this exact scenario (abandonment) is what I have been avoiding my entire life and it happened anyway despite my best efforts ... in the most unlikely of people.

Thankfully, after doing months of self-work, I was able to recall that past life story, and I worked hard to resolve that and all of the other abandonment issues, too. I mean, of course it's not their fault, but I felt like my grandfather and my uncle "abandoned" me with their passing.

Because I see how that fear from my past life – and even as a child, when something bad happened – had colored my decisions in my relationships in my entire adult life ...

I realized why I chose the relationships that I have ...

It was for my own self-preservation and protection. I loved the best that I knew how at the time.

I evolved and grew as a person throughout and after my divorce, and then certain events happened in the world such as the pandemic and certain racial horrors in our country, and I went to my ethical roots and drew upon that when looking for partners in the dating scene.

But low and behold, there is a divine, higher presence, wisdom, and guidance that puts certain people into our lives for our own soul growth ... and I also happen to believe God has a sense of humor!

I understand now that it's okay to feel your emotions, but not okay to let people walk all over you for fear that you will lose them.

The truth is, you can do everything right and they still have free will ... they can still leave you or cheat on you.

To cope and thrive, you have to be able to mourn loss and move on instead of letting it linger and break you.

As tragic and painful as it was for this ordeal to have happened to me – these people betraying me – these people I truly cared about and I thought had my back – and someone I really cared about that I thought I may have had a chance at a future with ... at least I put myself back together, learned a lot, and I now have the security that I will never make those same mistakes again.

LESSON: I must let the fear of loss go, because death and loss are inevitable, so I must focus on and cherish the love that I feel, that I have right before me while I can, right now in the moment that I am given and blessed with as the gift that it is, that's why it's called "the Present."

Trust

Stephan Labossiere a.k.a "Stephan Speaks" says that trust CAN be rebuilt. The formula is:

Time + Consistency

I believe this also. This is why I was giving her all those weeks and months to do exactly that – rebuild our friendship. I was giving her chances over and over again.

All I ever wanted was for her to acknowledge and apologize for her breach of trust.

To empathize with my feelings, and vow to always be transparent with me from now on.

Unfortunately, she was consistently lying and keeping information from me, then denying it, over and over again.

That is the only reason I had to end the relationship, which hurts me to this day.

Trust was the one thing that I didn't have for her in all of this since it was broken from the start.

I didn't entirely trust him, either, because I didn't really know him.

Now, I know better how to handle the issue of trust in my next relationship if I get a chance at one.

The issue of trust is handled in one way only = trusting myself.

I now trust myself to know exactly what it is I want and what I do not want.

I now trust myself to communicate my needs, wants, boundaries, and expectations to my future partner.

I now trust myself to speak up when my boundaries are being crossed or my needs aren't being met and making a request for those things.

I now trust myself to walk away from a relationship when those requests aren't being fulfilled.

LESSON: Trust yourself. Know your boundaries, wants, needs, and expectations; communicate them to your partner early on; make requests when a boundary is crossed or a need unmet; walk away when those requests are unfulfilled.

When you trust and know yourself well, this type of knowledge and communication is how you keep yourself safe in relationships = by creating health and well-being in them via open dialogue and understanding, in order to create happier, healthier connections that deepen over time.

Forgiveness

A COMPREHENSIVE DEFINITION OF forgiveness published in an article in "Greater Good Magazine: Science-Based Insights for a Meaningful Life," states:

> Psychologists generally define forgiveness as a conscious, deliberate decision to release feelings of resentment or vengeance toward a person or group who has harmed you, regardless of whether they actually deserve your forgiveness.

> Just as important as defining what forgiveness is, though, is understanding what forgiveness is not. Experts who study or teach forgiveness make clear that when you forgive, you do not gloss over or deny the seriousness of an offense against you. Forgiveness does not mean forgetting, nor does it mean condoning or excusing offenses. Though forgiveness can help repair a damaged relationship, it doesn't obligate you to reconcile with the person who harmed you, or release them from legal accountability.

> Instead, forgiveness brings the forgiver peace of mind and frees him or her from corrosive anger. While there is some debate over whether true forgiveness requires positive feelings toward the offender, experts agree that it at least involves letting go of deeply held negative feelings. In that

way, it empowers you to recognize the pain you suffered without letting that pain define you, enabling you to heal and move on with your life.

https://greatergood.berkeley.edu/topic/forgiveness/definition

This is exactly why I needed to let them both know in my last correspondence to them that I forgive them – in order to not let this pain define me, but to enable me to heal and move on with my life.

I still want to believe in my heart that most of the time she just didn't think when she said most of those hurtful things, because she's kind of quirky that way – it's part of her charm, and I do the same sometimes – we all say things that come out the wrong way. I understand and forgive her.

The times when she admitted she said stuff to purposely hurt me, I'm just going to believe that it was in retaliation because she was already hurting inside and jealous, and that her "I'm sorry for everything," means that she really is. My boundary is that I am no longer her doormat.

I wish her only peace, continued healing, and all good things for her and her family.

After reviewing this entire situation in the writing of this book – re-reading all her words in the screenshots I kept of her messages and texts … I feel her Spirit better now.

Now that more time has passed to distance myself from the trauma that she inflicted with her betrayal of my confidential conversations with her – as they say – hindsight is always 20/20 …

I know, like REALLY know deep down that the whole time she lied and kept information from me was because she didn't want to hurt my feelings.

I really and truly believe that now …

Except for the times she said the horrible, cutting words exclusively TO hurt my feelings, as she admitted, of course, but she did that because SHE was feeling hurt.

I get it.

We ALL do this.

It's human nature, normal, and I can't have the audacity to fault her for it, because I have done the same, no doubt.

And, because so much time has passed, I'm able to breathe and remember the good times, too.

How we always laughed and had fun together. We had the same sense of humor, the same lightness, the same personality. We even looked and acted enough alike that people mistook us for sisters. Towards the end, we seemed to have gotten that remark so many times, I just went with it. When they'd ask, I would reply, "Yeah, we are!" But, of course, I would correct them later and we would all laugh.

I have her to thank that my daughter recalls fond memories with her on the roller coasters at Cedar Point when we went with her and her sons that fall, which we were looking forward to making a regular event for us all.

It was because of her that I was able to create my volleyball team I love so much. I fact, we named it from a list she found online, and she liked that name the best.

It was because of her that I got back into bowling. We were going to be on a team together the following year, but then she had her second major health issue.

It was because of her that I got into karaoke that I love so much, and I found a whole new "karaoke family" to enjoy.

It was because of her that I met someone who changed my life, my perspective, and given me so much strength.

She gave me a beautiful "Journey" bracelet with a compass charm for being "On the Journey" that I like to wear and always remember her to this day.

She taught me to always keep a Sharpie in my purse. It has come in handy more than once! So, when I find I need to use it, I think of her.

I was so incredibly grateful when she came back into my life the year after my divorce was final. I wish she had been there the whole time, but we had a stupid falling out which was completely my fault 10 years prior.

I was a "perfectionist new mom," and I got mad at her at my son's Naming Ceremony, because her son was running around, and I felt she was being irresponsible and not watching him properly. I was so thoroughly stressed during those days, wanting everything to be perfect.

When we got in touch again, I apologized to her best I could, she forgave me, and our friendship had resumed stronger than ever.

… until he came along.

I remember many times she tried to ease my insecurities by telling me to have more confidence.

She just didn't understand that when people have past relationship trauma, as I did, it's not that easy to do.

I thank her for introducing me to him.

I don't regret one single moment with him.

The main problem he and I had was that he was 100% correct when he said in that message to our male mutual friend that she shouldn't've been involved.

I am happy she at least showed some kind of remorse and apologized in the best way she could, saying "I'm sorry for everything."

I do hope, however, that she also apologized to him, too, for having him lose a good woman in me.

Yet, my feeling is that his ex before me was most likely a good woman, too. She was in the military, so I have much respect for her already in that regard.

Interestingly, he never wanted to speak of her whatsoever. He never spoke of the dynamic of their relationship at all with me. I had no clue about their history.

The most I can remember is that I thought I heard that they were together for either 3 or 4 years. That's a long time! I bet she took a lot from him, poor thing.

He told me that they split because she cheated on him, and he thinks more than once. Plus, he believed she was "crazy" and "toxic," he said.

I recall when I was at his house, she called him a couple of times. We'd be on his couch, and I'd see her number come up on his phone and he'd just glance at it and look away. I told him he should answer it – that I didn't mind if he talked to her – it was okay with me. But, he said he "didn't want to hear the same old bull$#!+" from her and that he'd call her back later.

I made the mistake of mentioning these calls to her the second time it happened, and, as usual, she had something downright awful to say to me ... she goes ...

"Well, I know that they were sleeping together last year, even though they were still broken up. He went over there to get some of his things, and she made him dinner. So, I don't know what to tell you!"

Did she really need to tell me all of that? = No.

Did I ask? = No.

Was it any of my business? = No.

In hindsight, I can hardly call him my "ex," anyways, since we were only "Facebook Official," for all of about two weeks and then only the "Situationship" after that.

I was simply too afraid back then to give it my all.

I just wasn't ready.

By the time I figured myself out, it was too late.

I have done my work to forgive my ex-husband long ago, too. I have no bad juju towards him. I am committed to co-parenting with him in peace – for my kids' sake. I strive to keep him informed on all things concerning our children and maintain open communication on all things involving them.

My personality aspects still irritate him, and vice versa, but it's better and more manageable not living under the same roof and keeping a respectful personal distance.

I know he will be the only other person in the world who loves our kids as much as I do and who will always care for them more than any other man I will ever be with, as it should be.

Thus, I always respect and support my kids' relationship with their father, despite him not returning the same courtesy, but his behavior is no longer my concern. I am only responsible for my own behavior in raising my children.

Bottom line is ...

I don't hate anyone.

I forgive everyone.

I forgive her.

I forgive him.

And I certainly don't wish anything bad on anyone.

Most importantly, I forgive myself.

I can hold my head high knowing I would never be a person who would do the things to another person that they have done to me. My Karma is clean.

I love this Hawaiian "forgiveness prayer" called "Ho'oponopono."

> The word "ho'oponopono" roughly translates to "cause things to move back in balance" or to "make things right." It's a very Zen-like concept. (In native Hawaiian language, "pono" means balance, in the sense of "life." When things are in balance, nothing is off, so to speak.)
>
> https://graceandlightness.com/hooponopono-for-forgiveness/

Although there are several versions of this online, it goes like this:

I'm sorry
Please forgive me
Thank you
I love you

Repeating this as a mantra is very cleansing and helpful, to clear away negative energies. I highly recommend it.

LESSON: Forgiving our exes is a huge part of being healed and ready for a relationship. Make sure you've done your work before getting involved with someone. Don't think that a new relationship will solve your old wounds, because it won't – you'll just end up bleeding those old wounds onto the new person.

My Healing Journey

From "Finding Love After Heartbreak" by Stephan Lebossiere, Page 17:

> "On your personal path to healing, you must commit to doing the work it takes to process through any unresolved pain and hurt lingering from your past."

After the "ghosting," I dove headlong into what I termed "My Healing Journey," and did everything possible to help myself heal.

Below, I'm sharing all of the workshops, books, movies, and activities I've done.

Books:

- "Finding Love After Heartbreak" by Stephan Lebossiere, a.k.a. "Stephan Speaks"
- "The Man God Has For Me" by Stephan Lebossiere
- "I Choose Me" by Cynthia James
- "The 21-Day Loving Me Challenge" book by Shakira Taylor (and subscribed to her YouTube channel)
- "Who Have You Come Here to Be? 101 Possibilities for Contemplation" by Rima Bonario, Jane Simmons and Kelly Isola

- "Move Beyond the Block" by La'Keisha Gray-Sewell
- "Fearless Women: Visions of a New World" by Mary Ann Halpin
- Calling In The One" 7-week workshop by Katherine Woodward Thomas
- "Love People, Use Things" by "The Minimalists," Joshua Fields Millburn & Ryan Nicodemus
- "Codependent No More" by Melody Beattie
- "You Can Heal Your Heart" by Louise Hay
- "Mirror, Mirror" by Sunni Boheme
- "Help. Thanks. Wow." by Anne Lamont
- "The Soulmate Process" by Bob Lancer
- "Living Untethered – Beyond the Human Predicament" by Michael A. Singer church study group
- "The Untethered Soul" by Michael A. Singer
- "The Prospering Power of Love" by Catherine Ponder

Workshops/Classes:

- "Relationship Goals" 8-Week Series by Pastor Michael Todd (Transformation Church)
- "Pray for Your Future Spouse" 5-day workshop (The One University with Jamal & Natasha Miller)
- "Grief, Loss & Change" 6-week class at Unity of Fox Valley Church
- "New Beginnings Group (NBG)" 60-day program with Trent Shelton

- "Illuminate the Darkness 5 Day Journey" by Briana Borten
- "Blueprints for Positive Change: Become the Architect of Your Life" church retreat (Leader also did healing physical work on me.)
- "Be Like Water" Workshop at church by Daniel Nahmod

Spiritual Movies/Videos:

- Dr. Strange
- Collateral Beauty
- The Shack
- The Wisdom Tree
- Birdman
- Captain Fantastic
- The Celestine Prophesy
- Peaceful Warrior
- Journey to Betterment
- What the Bleep Do We Know?
- Heal Your Life by Louise Hay
- Ambition to Meaning (the Shift) by Dr. Wayne Dyer
- "The Art of Being Extraordinary" lecture with Dr. Wayne Dyer & Eckhart Tolle
- Re-watched my entire collection of GOLD Rush Women's Conference series on DVD
- Subscribed to "Stephan Speaks" YouTube channel
- Subscribed to Matthew Coast's YouTube channel
- Subscribed to Matthew Hussy's YouTube channel
- Subscribed to Jay Shetty's YouTube channel

Soulmate Movies:

- Cloud Atlas
- A Winter's Tale
- Two of a Kind
- What Dreams May Come
- Ghost
- Somewhere in Time
- The Secret: Dare to Dream

Audio Books:

- The Camino by Shirley MacLaine
- This Naked Mind by Annie Grace
- Never Eat Alone by Keith Ferrazzi
- Radical Forgiveness by Colin Tipping

Activities:

- Started a new journal day after Memorial Day weekend
- Started a bowling team with my mom and two friends.
- Participated in "Sober October" (10/2-11/1/22)
- Participated in "AF April" (3/24-5/2/23)
- Participated in "40 Days of Letting Go" Lent booklet
- Cord Cutting with Archangel Michael Meditation
- Began "Psychic Oz" readings
- Akashic Records Reading by a friend

- Joined Matthew Coast's "Relationship Advice for Women - The Goddess Community" Facebook group
- Joined TGIF Meetup group
- Changed work passwords to a new positive phrase
- St. Raphael the Archangel Novena - Healing Prayers
- Night Nation Run at Soldier Field/McCormick Place
- Finished my Def Leppard "Hysteria" album cover puzzle I got as a gift from my cousin back in December 2000
- Completed testing and received my Brown/Red Karate belt in Hapkido/Tung Soo Do
- Began to pursuing dating options
- Made the decision to start writing this book for soul healing and release of the situation
- Digitized all my artwork and decided to frame my favorites and display them

I also kept track of all "Epiphanies" I've had throughout this healing journey. Here are a few I'm able to share:

- My Native American warrior from my past life had to leave me to teach me to understand and believe how strong I am; that I can thrive without him.
- A part of me feels ashamed about being divorced. I feel like I "should" be married to make my Mom happy and have her not worry about me, like I failed my kids and my ex-husband, and I often

wonder why I am not "worthy" of any other man wanting to be my husband and have a secure life again.

- What happened with "him" could be my karma for not taking my long-term ex-boyfriend seriously, because I didn't consider him to be "husband material."

- I'M technically the one who broke up with HIM the day after that night he walked away, instead of talking to him, if what he said is true that "he wasn't even mad the next day."

- I'M the one who blocked HIM first instead of talking to him when I saw her message about them both saying things to purposely upset me.

- I drove him away because I forgot who I was and didn't act my best. He needed me to be the Queen that I am, but instead, I lost myself in my insecurities, past relationship trauma, and "Anxious Attachment" relationship style.

- I have a tendency to approach new relationships and dating already angry and defensive. I look for red flags right away in order to end the relationship quickly, before I get too involved and get hurt.

- Because I was angry and defensive with this one ("him") from the start (and much of the time) due to my own issues, I was already convinced of what I thought I knew, instead of talking to him – just like he did to me at the end.

- In this situation, I just needed the truth, and to be heard with love, empathy, and respect.

- He wasn't the one hurting me all that time with his silence – I was. (By my thoughts.)
- She didn't lie to me and keep information from me to be mean – she did it to protect my feelings.
- If it weren't for him being friends with her, he never would have met me. Aside from what happened between them, he "friend-zoned" her decades ago. Thus, I believe he sincerely considers her just his "sister," as he told me, and nothing more.
- I was keeping secrets, too = 1. I never told him about my feelings for him. 2. I never told him the things she was saying to me and our mutual friends.
- This all happened for me to write this book, and most importantly, to learn this:
  1. Know my worth
  2. Tell people what I need from them
  3. Tell people how I feel

- I now understand the definition of a "hot mess."

LESSON: Do the work it takes to process through any unresolved pain and hurt lingering from your past. Even if you are already in a relationship now, doing this is an incredibly healthy experience.

Gratitude

I ALWAYS START MY "Guru" books with the chapter "An Attitude of Gratitude," but this time, I'm ending this section with simply "Gratitude."

My dear Buddhist friend says I need to reframe my attitude that all this happened "for" me, not "to" me.

I believe that this happened so I could write this book.

It happened so that I could heal myself and help others.

With me and him, we both were just not ready for each other.

Both of our baggage was way too much.

Having her in the middle was a complete disaster – THAT was what "never should have happened."

But on the other hand, I know and understand she was correct that everything happens for a reason.

In fact, I need to consider that she did me a favor. I need to consider the distinct possibility that perhaps he is a man who just does this to women, and that he would eventually have done this to me down the road over anything and it would have been ten times worse.

Therefore, it is probably a blessing that we never got the fresh start that we both talked about deserving towards the end.

In reviewing all the emails and screenshots, remembering everything that has happened …

I see clearly that this "Situationship" needed to end.

For all concerned.

I can't imagine how stressful it must have been for him hearing all this stuff about me from her all the time while trying to focus on a new job out of state.

It's too bad he didn't appreciate that I never brought him my problems that didn't have anything to do with him during that time. On the contrary, I respected his time and stress level, because I am a strong, independent woman who can handle any of my issues with people on my own.

In that regard, it makes sense that he did the right thing for himself by getting himself out of the situation entirely – albeit to my detriment at the time.

Now, I am entirely grateful to no longer have anyone in my life to cause me such pain.

If they can't act right and treat me right, then they are doing me a favor by just leaving me alone.

Sometimes, in cases like these, when people leave your life, it is for the best. It means they don't love you and aren't willing to care for you and treat you the proper way that you deserve to be treated.

Obviously, I didn't have my boundaries in place then to stop their abuse myself.

Now I clearly see everything that happened, and I know something like this will never happen to me again.

That's why it was so important for me to write this book. To help others in my position to either stop their pain or prevent it from ever happening like it happened to me.

I do hope my kids read this someday when they are older and in relationships to help them as well.

I hope my daughter never experiences this kind of treatment and I hope my son is a better man than the ones I've had to deal with.

Alas, his decision and treatment towards me being so dehumanizing and traumatic was exactly the impetus I needed to delve into myself and dig out all the past pain, baggage, lessons, and other junk in my brain and heart to heal and release it once and for all.

I probably would not have done this much work on myself, nor ever written this book for others if it all hadn't happened exactly the way God had intended it to happen.

Healing, forgiveness, and moving on with my life has been my focus ever since.

LESSON: Make lemonade out of lemons. Being grateful for what you have feels better than crying over what you don't have.

Getting Back Out There Again

Sugar

THIS AND THE FOLLOWING chapters are purely for entertainment purposes.

We can all learn lessons every day of our lives in everything we do, but I'm including this part to simply share my experiences I've had since the ghosting.

I want my readers and those who care about me to know I didn't just crawl in my room and hide when it happened, but instead, I did my best to get back out there in tandem with doing all that work I listed above in "My Healing Journey" chapter.

Those in my dedication already know this, but for those who may know me, but don't know all this that happened to me, I am reassuring you that I kept working on healing myself and continuing to give other men chances.

My Southern friend calls kisses getting some "sugar." This reference also reminds me of my favorite song of all time, "Pour Some Sugar On Me" by my favorite band of all time, Def Leppard.

As part of my healing journey, I kept a list of men I've kissed since the ghosting. The lucky number is 13 as of the time of this writing.

This was done purely for the purpose of rebuilding my confidence to know and remember that I am still attractive to men.

The number of men who wished me a "Happy Mother's Day" this year was 12. I kept this list not for my "attractiveness quota" (my ego), but as proof that there are still kind, considerate, respectful men out there who like me for more than just the way I look – that they are thinking of me and respect me as a mother. This is important to me, as I am working on trusting men again, so this was an exercise I needed to do to help me with that.

I am doing my best to carve the names of the ones who do right by me in stone, and the ones who do wrong by me in sand.

The Next One

I WAS A PART of a Facebook group that organized events. Originally when I joined pre-pandemic, it was a type of singles group, but then a lot of couples formed in it, so it changed to just be more of a "party" group.

About a month after the ghosting, I posted that I was going to a local concert and invited anyone to come hang. So, a couple guys from that group met up with me there. I hit it off with one of them who was tall, fit (had terrific muscles!), and rode a Harley.

We discussed our fitness routines, diets, music, his bike, parenting, and other things we enjoyed doing.

We shared a kiss goodnight, which was my first since "him," then we became Facebook friends.

We messaged for probably about a week when he decided he was still in love with his ex.

Thankfully, I already asked some girls in the group about him, so I was duly warned via "Girl Code" he'd been on-and-off with her, and therefore, I wasn't heartbroken, just a little disappointed.

Bumble Lunch Date

THIS GUY AND I agreed to meet up at a restaurant for dinner about an hour north of me, because he lived pretty far. We were messaging pretty steadily, but didn't video chat yet. I wanted to be taken out on a proper date, and he offered, so I was really looking forward to this.

The day comes and about 4:00 he lets me know that he wasn't feeling well – that he thinks he got food poisoning and asked to reschedule us for the following week (due to my parenting schedule), and I agreed.

We messaged a bit throughout the week, and then the day came to meet up.

I messaged him at lunch joking that he should be careful what he eats, and he thought it was funny and we were still on.

I got all ready and hopped on the app to tell him I was on my way.

I discovered he'd deleted his account.

The Dancer

ONE NIGHT I WAS seeing my friend's band perform and this guy who had been eying me all night came up to where I was dancing in front of the stage and started to dance with me.

I allowed it and then went back to where he was sitting to talk with him a bit and I really liked him.

We became Facebook friends and started chatting for the next week.

He finally asked me out to dinner, and I agreed, looking forward to seeing him again.

The day came we were going to have dinner, and I jumped on Messenger to discover that he was no longer there. Either he blocked me or had deleted his account.

I never heard from him again.

Volleyball Fun

THERE WAS A VERY young guy (just around where Gen Z and Millennial meet) on another team in one of my volleyball leagues (I was in two at this point), that I was totally crushing on. Now that I had no ties, I figured I'd put my flirt on full volume one night playing pickup and see what happened – well, it worked … turned out he was attracted to me, too!

We had a great conversation, shared kisses a time or two, and then by the third or 4th week, he told me he was getting back with his ex.

I was totally okay with that, however, because he was way too young for me, anyway, and thus I had no hard feelings.

Besides, I kissed his other equally young handsome friend after our pickup games one week, too, although that ended up being a one-time thing.

The point of sharing this experience is that I felt totally amazing that guys in their 20's are finding me attractive! I felt my confidence coming back, reminding me of when I was involved with Adonis, but even better because they were even younger than he is now!

The Construction Worker

THERE IS A PLACE within 5 minutes of the venue that hosted my Wednesday night volleyball games that used to be called "Aurora's Tiki Hut," that I had learned about too late, because they since had new owners and removed the name "Aurora," to my dismay.

It's now called "The Beach Hut."

Ugh.

I decided I needed to visit one night when I was in the area after an early game …

First, I stopped at the local brewery where I am a "Beer Club of the Month" member (long story behind that, as I enjoy "Jesus' Preferred Beverage" – wine!) to pick up my beer-of-the-month and interact with the staff and anyone else I knew there.

So, I'm at the counter, re-watching a live video that my teammate recorded of our games that night (~45 minutes total), when this hot guy comes up next to me and asks me what I'm watching.

I did see him out of the corner of my eye staring at me, but I'm used to that, so I just ignored it, as always.

His having the bravery to approach me impressed me.

I love confidence in a man.

So, I show him and explain about my volleyball team and that I was actually meeting my teammate and his wife at "Aurora's Tiki Hut" just after I finish my beer.

He says he wants to follow.

I said, great!

I leave and go there.

He literally shows up.

Wow.

I'm impressed he kept his word.

He seemed he was quite "relaxed" already at the other place, so I was expecting he'd never show.

Thankfully, my teammate and his wife were already there and saved me a table, so when this guy walked in with me, we both had a seat.

I made the polite introductions, and it was a really nice time.

Being a "Tiki Hut," they were playing appropriate music ...

My Bob came on!!!!!!!

(Bob Marley = I am a HUGE fan – many great Bob music memories I can't even get into here ... contact me to discuss ...!)

Can't recall the exact song that came on when he asked me to dance ... maybe "One Love," because that seems to fit ...

So, I put my arms around his neck and ... MY GOD.

... the MUSCLES.

His upper arms, shoulders, neck, upper back were ROCK SOLID.

Because this touch seemed familiar to me, I had to ask ...

"What do you do for a living?"

He replied, "Construction. Concrete."

OMG.

That is the exact profession "He" was in!!!!

Wow.

We exchanged numbers.

He was wise and didn't drive there ... he lived close enough that he could skateboard.

And, he was around my age! So, he asked me if I could take him home and I said yes.

We pulled in his driveway and he said to try and be quiet ... of which I knew was a red flag right away.

I asked why.

He said because his wife may hear.

S.O.B.!!!

I went in on him and he defended himself saying that she's never around and he's always home watching the kids, because he works different shifts than her and that it's a living hell and yadda, yadda, yadda …

… the same reasons all these other guys give me as an excuse to stay in a loveless marriage.

… and they expect ME to be sympathetic …

When I've lost EVERYTHING getting my divorce …

No, thank you.

I have NO sympathy left when YOU choose to stay miserable.

Sorry.

Not happening.

I got home and looked him up on Facebook.

Yes, he certainly was married.

Burned again.

Deleted his number that I had just programmed earlier.

Another one bites the dust.

California Harley Guy

OF ALL THE DATING sites, I really enjoy Facebook dating the best, because I feel safer that they are a real person, and I can see if we have any mutual friends, of which I could glean more information on him from, if possible.

This really helped me in the case of this guy. He seemed SO sweet and chill and he was not playing games – he, too, was looking for a life partner and was eager to meet me right away instead of playing "pen pal," which gets on my nerves.

We met at one of my favorite breweries for a quick afternoon beer before a local parade that was about to start. We had a great conversation and since the parade was just a couple of miles away, he wanted to drive us there on his Harley.

I was nervous, because I hadn't been on a motorcycle since I was a teenager and my uncle drove me around the city block a time or two on his. However, I agreed, and it was amazing!

We had a quick snack, watched the parade, and then had dinner together at a place where my friend was performing nearby. Some other friends where there, so we sat with them and had a great time.

Things were going SO well we still didn't want to say goodbye, so I invited him out to a place where I do karaoke and then we kissed goodbye.

The next day he asked me out again, and I agreed.

We were messaging all week, and it was going well. I was SO excited to see him again.

The day of the date came and around 10:30, he messaged me that he forgot he had an appointment for his new puppy and asked to reschedule.

I said no. I had been burned too many times with these guys flaking on me and I said that I will not be rescheduling with him, because I was looking forward to this date all week.

He should have checked his calendar before even asking me on the date to make sure he was available and blocked out his time for me.

I need a man I can count on. If he's flaking on me now, he'll do it in the future, and that's just not what I'm looking for.

I'm learning what my boundaries are and sticking to them.

He was upset, but oh well.

The Garbage Man

THIS GENTLEMAN WAS ANOTHER Facebook Dating find. He was modestly handsome, but what I liked about him most was that he was also willing to just meet out right away instead of messaging too much.

We casually met for the first time not as a "date," but I was somewhere local to him seeing another friend perform. He said he was already out with his friend and asked to come by. I said yes. He came by with his friend and we had a very nice conversation.

We kept messaging and decided to meet again. This time he came alone, and we saw a different friend of mine perform. It was also a casual meetup, not a date, but he bought me a drink this time. We danced together and it was really nice.

We parted ways with no kisses, because I wanted to take this one slow. I could tell he hadn't dated in a while and wasn't a player which was refreshing to me.

However, something in our conversation triggered my "Spidey-Sense," and I thought to ask the question if he was REALLY divorced or not … I didn't want to get caught up in another Eros situation.

Turns out that yes, it was similar to another Eros situation.

His wife walked out years ago, but they are not legally divorced. She lives nearby, but in this case, he barely sees her, and she has no interest in seeing him or being a proper mother to their son. He is the primary caregiver.

He said he didn't want to file for divorce, because he didn't want to deal with child support and wanted to continue keeping sole custody of his son, as it was.

He was such a kind, honest, hardworking man, but that was a dealbreaker for me, and so I told him so right then.

He understood and we parted ways peacefully.

I'm learning to ask better questions sooner and remain steadfast in sticking to my boundaries.

The Drummer

OKAY, SO THIS GUY was REALLY handsome! I met him on Facebook Dating. He was a drummer in a thrash metal band and tall – I mean like 6'4" or something crazy like that.

Anyway, we videochatted twice and he was a total sweetheart on top of it.

Suddenly, he unmatched us and I thought he was gone.

Until he sent me a friend request on Facebook a few months later! I accepted, but restricted, since I don't know him, but wanted to chat.

I told him I was surprised to hear from him, since he just cut it off like he did, and he said that he got off Facebook dating but had been "stalking" me ever since.

> Aurora!!!·.... I've been secretly stalking you for a while now. We had a couple video chats, and I believe that put you into my contacts ... somewhat. How are you doing? Looks like you're living your best life and still looking great doing it. I'm surviving.

I took his "stalking" comment as he was joking, and I wasn't scared, because I knew where to find him via his band's Facebook page – I could see everywhere he was playing – and because now I had access to his own personal page, I could see even more.

So, I continued messaging with him a few times while I checked out his page.

Turns out it looked like he had a girlfriend.

I asked him about her, he didn't reply, but unfriended me.

Busted! Who did he think he was fooling?

Joker!

The Creep

AT ONE OF THE local places that I frequent showcasing live music, I met another musician. This guy was older but seemed interesting to me. I wasn't attracted to him "in that way," but he sure had a lot of stories to tell.

I discovered we had a mutual friend. He gave me his card and asked for my number to keep in touch, so I did, thinking he was "safe," because he was clearly too old for me to date, so I figured we'd just be friends.

So, the next day, I must have missed his call, because I had a voice mail from a number I didn't know.

I listened to it and all I heard at first was, "Aurora ... Borealis ..." In this creepy voice.

I got chills.

He literally sounded like a murderer who was stalking me!

Then, he went on to the rest of his message in a bit more of a normal tone, but never stated who he was.

I was SO creeped out ... I'm thinking to myself, "Who the heck could this possibly be???"

Then, I remembered meeting him the night before and his card, so I checked – yes, the number was his.

Oh. My. God.

I didn't even want to reply, but I didn't want to be rude ... or worse ... have him keep calling me, so I programmed him and texted him.

It was okay at first. We talked about his music, and he sent me some audio clips to listen to.

But, over the days, things just got weird.

For some reason, he kept getting angry at me — misunderstanding what I was saying, telling me I should have come up to him and said hi, things like that. I had my friend walk me out because I was so creeped out by this guy when I saw him last.

And, he typed very strangely, I could barely figure out what he was saying, so that creeped me out as well.

I ended up having to block him.

Here was our last text exchange where he saw me out:

> So, I'm going to politely request that you please don't message me anymore.

O thouit it was didn't remember tho Omg

Now I'm afended u didn't come up to me to say hi
u left with him anyway so whats the dif

Goodbye

I've seen him socially since, but pretended not to, and I
make sure to sit with someone, so he won't approach me.

The Friend

So, I met this guy through a friend at a place I used to frequent. He was nice looking and seemed kind, but I wasn't really interested at the time.

However, I saw him out at another place, and we had a great conversation where he bought me a drink and we became Facebook friends.

I bumped into him at yet a third place shortly after that where we chatted, and he bought me a drink again and this time we exchanged numbers.

We were casually texting here and there until one night he asked what I was doing, and I happened to be seeing a band perform with another friend and her boyfriend and said he was welcome to come meet me there. He took me up on my offer and drove over a half hour from where we lived to see me (we live close).

We had a great evening getting to know each other better, he bought me a couple of drinks this time, talked to my friends, and we even danced together up front near the band. He asked me to drive him to his car (which, I thought was strange, since it was in the same parking lot), but nothing happened when we said goodnight, he didn't try anything – it was just friendly.

I was really beginning to like this guy and felt he liked me, too. I loved how respectful he was – he wasn't being too forward and taking things slow.

So, I decided to hunt around on his Facebook page ... his status didn't say anything, but looked like he has a girlfriend of which he never mentioned once in all the time we've chatted, met up, and him buying me drinks.

I let it go until he reached out to me again, which he did a few days later.

I'll let the text exchange speak for itself:

A friend has extra tickets to a baseball game tonight. Would you want to go?

I already have plans, but thank you for thinking of me.

OK

It appears, however, that you're romantically involved with your business colleague.

That said, I don't feel comfortable going on dates with you.

But if the day comes you're completely single, I'd be interested.

Thanks, and see you around!

I wasn't asking you on a date, just offering you a ticket to a baseball game. I told her I asked you to go. I'm not being deceptive, just trying to be a friend.

Thanks, no worries, take care!

I think you got things a little wrong I wasn't asking you on a date a friend won 6 tickets to the baseball game and you love to do everything so you were the first person I thought of who would like to go. I only asked because we have fun together and it hurts my feelings that you think...

... and blah, blah, blah ... because, now *I* was the one hurting *his* feelings, apparently ...

I apologized for hurting his feelings, and never heard from him again.

I haven't seen him around since, and eventually, I unfriended him.

No hard feelings, there's just nothing more to say here.

Another one bites the dust.

The Mirage

A HANDSOME FACE CAUGHT my eye one evening in my Facebook feed's "People You May Know" ribbon.

I checked out his profile and was really impressed. He was so good looking, a proud father, and wore a huge silver cross on his chest, which told me he was a Christian, like me, even though that's not a must-have, but nice to have a man of Faith, for a change. It makes life easier.

On top of it, in his profile picture, he was wearing a shirt that was my favorite color – light blue – with a background that matched. I felt it was a sign.

I never become Facebook friends with anyone I haven't met in person yet, so I let it go.

About a month or so later, I was a part of another Facebook travel group and somehow, I spotted his name in the group, and I couldn't believe my eyes – it was him!

I checked out his profile to see if we had any mutual friends and we did!

So, I decided to just send him a message in Messenger, because you can do that with folks even if you're not Facebook friends, and it just goes in their "Message Request" folder. That's the best I could do – hope he sees it and responds, but he never did.

So, I asked two of our mutual friends about him and only one got back to me. Turns out this guy also frequented a place I did, but on a night that I had my kids. So, although I couldn't go there on that night he did, I kept going to see if someday I would bump into him, but I never did.

I asked the mutual friend to please just tell him about me and see what happens. This guy also worked at a nearby place and told me to just go there when he's working, but the hours just didn't work for me.

Yet, I took his advice and did try to go there about 3-4 times, but every time I went, he wasn't working.

I kept checking the message I sent him to see if he even read it – he never did. The mutual friend told me he's barely ever on Facebook, anyways, so I guess that was a bust.

Lo and behold, however, when I was on vacation for my birthday, it turns out that I posted and tagged a picture of a person I didn't even realize was a mutual friend of ours and he "liked" the picture! I was thrilled!

A couple of days later, he sent me a Friend request – ON my birthday!!! I accepted – without restricting this time – figuring this was God's birthday gift to me!

I was hoping that perhaps now that we're Facebook friends, he'd seen my message in his Messenger, and reach out to me.

He never did.

He never even "liked" or commented on any of my posts, and he didn't post anything I could "like" or comment on. I didn't want to be a stalker and go reacting or commenting on his past posts.

So, after a couple of weeks, I unfriended him.

If he were interested, he would have reached out, or "liked" or commented on my posts. I mean, he sent me a friend request for a reason, right?

If he was just a stalker and wanted to see all this information about me, but not reach out, well, that was creepy to me.

I don't play games like that.

Never heard from the guy.

"It was only just a dream," as Nelly would say …

Ethically Non-Monogamous

AT THIS POINT, I was feeling healed, braver, and more secure in my decisions, given this craziness that's been happening with these past few men. So, I decided to pay for a one-month subscription to OK Cupid – my old favorite! I figured I was ready and willing to see what happens, giving it a more serious try again.

I chatted with several guys, and one I was interested in that I had been chatting with a few days, I come to find he is into being monogamous while he enjoys his female partners to be "ethically non-monogamous."

He said it "excites him" to know she is sleeping with other men while he remains faithful.

I told him that's not for me, wished him luck, and unmatched us.

A Medical Experiment

STILL ON OK CUPID, I was being more open-minded about my age preferences and decided to match with men in their 30's after all.

I was chatting with this one and suddenly he goes "Oh, I forgot to ask you ... are you vaccinated against COVID?"

I proudly replied that I was and that I was also boosted and my kids too, figuring he was pro-vaccine, and that it was important to him.

His reply to me was, "Oh, well, I don't date women that are vaccinated. I don't participate in medical experiments."

So, I go, "Oh, ok, take care then," and I unmatched us.

Unrealistic

RIGHT AWAY, I CAN'T stand when guys put a fake name on their profile, but I was trying to be more open-minded, giving this a real chance, still.

This one went by "Blu". Ugh.

Well, it was my favorite color, although spelled wrong, and so I gave it a shot.

I kept the transcript that goes like this:

Hi. How's things?

> Just home chilling now!

Me too. Bedtime actually

> Yup! Chat tomorrow! Goodnight!

Ok. Night

> Hope we can message more tomorrow, ok?
> Hey, in the meantime.... let me know what you're looking for in the way of your ideal relationship.

At this stage in life with everyone set in there ways and having life limitations I doubt any of us will find our "ideal " relationship. Not very realistic I don't think.

Okay, good luck and take care! :)

This is crazy stuff I answer one question and you say good bye. Funny world we live in

Well, if you don't believe in an ideal relationship, there is no point.
I didn't say perfect person – it's who is willing to at least try.

His response was too negative, saying that "everyone is set in their ways" and "life limitations," doubting "anyone will find their ideal relationship," saying it's unrealistic.

I want someone who is willing to try. To put the work in for an amazing, fun, fulfilling relationship. It takes two people willing to give it their all.

Friend of the Family

ANOTHER OK CUPID ONE, just a couple years older than me. This man was SO incredibly kind and genuine! He was attractive, and in chatting, I got a good feeling about him.

So, I set up a Zoom chat with him, giving him a link to my private Zoom account. This man had never "Zoomed" before, so it was charming that I had to help him learn how to install the program (with the help of a friend of his, he said) so that he could do his first "Zoom date" with me. I learned how to "Zoom date" over the pandemic and had become quite proficient at it.

After some "technical difficulties" getting started, I was pleased to see that he was true to his pictures.

Fortunately, this man was an open book and told me his story about how he ended up on a dating site and I briefly told him mine.

Unfortunately, he was newly broken up with this woman just over a month, whom he'd been with for over two years who screwed him over by staying married to her husband and still living in the house with him, when she kept telling him she was going to leave him.

Poor guy! That is EXACTLY why I never date men who are in a "bad relationship" planning on getting divorced, or newly broken up, or "separated," etc., as I mentioned before.

However, I recognized right away – exactly like Desmond did for me – that this man was not ready for what I needed.

Plus, it seemed as if he hadn't been on his own (single) at all – that he just kept going from one relationship to the next. It didn't sit well with me. I'm looking for someone who knows how to be on their own, like me.

He seemed too eager to be with someone and not enough of his own man, his own person.

I kept my response to him, because I thought it was pretty good and just in case I have to do this in the future, I wouldn't have to re-write too much for the next one, so I'll share it here:

> (Name), you seem very nice – you're attractive, you're true to your pictures, and at this point, I have no reason to believe you're lying about anything.
>
> That said, I believe every word you're saying about your ex and because of that, I feel (from my own personal experience), that your breakup is way too soon to try and date unless it's casual, but you and I agreed we're looking for the "rest of our lives" person.

Thus, may I humbly suggest you do what I did and give yourself the rest of this year to "get back to You," and heal from your back-to-back divorce and breakup and moving back home on top of it … all this in a very recent time.

It sucks to be alone - especially for caring, kind, thoughtful, emotional people such as ourselves, but it's necessary.

It's necessary for yourself and to get back to your roots and who you are - set your own boundaries and standards so that you'll never again let a woman jerk you around for years, months at a time, placing you second-best when you have so much to offer.

I hear what you're saying about moving forward and that's great, but you owe it to yourself and your future woman to take a breather first – to stabilize. There's nothing wrong with a little time and everything to gain.

Believe me when I say it's not easy, but it's worth it.

God Bless and take care! :)

His response:

I understand, and I thank you for the positivity. I really do appreciate that.

Well, after that, I was done. That was it for me.

That was the last one I bothered messaging with on this site. I stopped matching myself with anyone, let my one-month subscription run out, and removed my credit card, so that it didn't automatically renew.

I officially cancelled my OK Cupid membership, set my account as "Taking a Break" from Facebook Dating, and haven't gone back on any dating sites since.

The Family Lunch

ONE FRIDAY NIGHT, I met this gorgeous young gentleman at a concert. He and his friend were in the military.

When I say gorgeous – I mean olive skin, blue eyes, black hair, killer smile. He wasn't tall, but he was perfectly proportioned and a great dancer.

Problem is, he had way too much to drink, although at least he knew it and apologized, and seemed so sincere that when he asked for my number, I gave it to him and told him to get in touch with me tomorrow after he sobers up and made his friend promise me he'd get him home safe.

That very night, he already texted me that he was home safe, which was nice.

The next day, Saturday, we texted back and forth and exchanged pictures and he asked me out to lunch after my church the next day, Sunday.

Later that night, however, he texted me that he's got a family lunch that he didn't know he had and asked if we could meet later or reschedule.

I asked him, "So, your family dictates what you do?"

He said that they were in town, and it was planned, and they said he had to be there.

Well, I said he should enjoy the lunch with his family, but I was no longer interested.

I mean, as you've read, this seems to keep happening to me.

Whether it was true or not, I've been through this too many times, and so my answer was no, and that was that.

The Date That Never Happened

MET THIS GENTLEMAN AT a place I used to frequent that had karaoke.

I stopped going there pretty much only because I stopped classes in the area.

However, he had taken an interest in me, and we had 3 important things in common:

1. He played pool
2. He sang karaoke
3. He was about my age

Plus, he was kind to my special friend that I also had met at karaoke. He said he loved how I interacted with my special friend and that warmed my heart, because he saw into mine.

We exchanged numbers and became Facebook friends.

Well, one day I happened upon a post he put up that suggested antisemitism, and I was utterly disgusted.

I raised my concerns to him via text, and he did his best to alleviate them and explain himself, but then I hadn't heard from him in months.

He finally reached out and said he felt bad that I was "scolding him" over my concerns:

> … and, why do you say I'm not a fan of yours??

> You scolded me about my post.

> So? I let you know how I felt about your post, that's all.

> I've been shamed

> I'm sorry I hurt your feelings, but it's just the way I feel about such things.
>
> I mean, if you're not, then just be mindful of what you post, so it's not misconstrued as such, that's all.

So, a couple weeks after that, he texted me to invite me to the local Corn Boil he's at, but I was already out with my daughter on other plans.

Then ... nearly TWO MONTHS later, he asks me to a Peter Gabriel concert at the United Center here in Chi-Town ...!!!

Um ...

I hadn't heard from this guy in months and now this??

I told him that was pretty bold, considering ...

Last I heard he was starting a new job to improve his situation (déjà vu!!) ...

> Why is that bold? I've mentioned I'd like to take you out.
> I've seen it advertised a lot of Facebook and I thought of you.
> I miss seeing you and I'd like to see more of you.
> I wish you'd come to the karaoke bar again.
>
> New job was a bust.
> Back to doing home improvements workin for myself.

Then, he asked me about the places I do karaoke in his area, because he then disclosed he got 2 DUI's and lost his license for 4 years and that he Ubers ...

Okay, I totally respect Ubering, no problem, but now we're in a text conversation arranging where to meet and when ... around him having to drink, since there's like NO mention of literally maybe going on a date where NOT drinking or only drinking in moderation is an option ... which is a HUGE red flag for me ...

Then, he DID offer to go out on a date with me without drinking – which was wonderful! So, he had my attention again.

Next, we text back-and-forth on how excited he is that a "hot chick" like me accepted a date with him, but then when I try to "lock it down," like an actual date and time ...

Crickets.

He asks me my availability and I tell him.

I admit that yes, being a single mom with split custody of my children severely deters my dating availability.

I suggest we meet after my Thursday night bowling league, and this is what I get:

> Wow you're quite the scheduler.
> Not much for seat of the pants runner I guess.
>
> Where do you bowl? (Thursday)

> No, not when you're
> a single mom of school-
> age children in activities
> who has cultivated
> a vital social life
> post-divorce!

.. and guess what …

I haven't heard from him since … as of this writing …

That was just over a week ago when he sent me that text last Sunday night.

I unfriended him.

Case closed.

The Skydiver

I WAS HAVING DINNER alone on a Sunday night before I had to get my kids from their Dad's, since it was his weekend at my local "Happy Place" on a gorgeous September evening.

Two guys and a girl came onto the patio and sat at the table in front of me. I wasn't sure if the one guy and girl were a couple, but the younger guy was definitely single, because I could see him turning around to check me out from the corner of my eye and whispering something to the other guy.

All of a sudden, the younger guy calls his friend on speakerphone, and he proceeds to ask the guy if he wanted to go skydiving on Thursday. He made a BIG production out of his conversation about it, making sure I could hear ... totally "peacocking" – it was hilarious!

Once he's done, the guy turns to me and asks me if I would like to go skydiving with him on Thursday.

I laughed and said absolutely not, but thanked him for the invite, and we all had a short conversation about skydiving, because apparently, he's been once, but liked it so much, he wants to go again.

Then, he asked the young waitress if she wanted to go and she said yes and they exchanged numbers, and I was glad, since she was clearly his age.

When I got up to leave, he asked me again if I was sure I didn't want to go and I confirmed. I was really flattered.

I thought it was a very clever way to pick up a woman and admired his creativity and boldness. However, I know for sure that I don't want a man that young, although many other women my age would say I was crazy, and that I should have gone for it.

When I was doing the online dating, I first had my preference set to the age range of 40-60, but despite that, these apps still let men outside that range select you.

Although I entertained a few that were younger, I got to the point I even increased my age range to 45-60, because I find that I'm honestly just not into younger men.

For one, they just make me feel old, and two, they can't relate to my 80's culture references and life circumstances such as kids and divorce.

Although, I didn't want to be a person to rule anyone out "on paper," I used to still click on guys who said something of substance in their profile and/or I feel an attraction to – so that I have something to start with, at least.

But, no more.

I'm so done with online, and I'm not going to date a man that young, because I know exactly what I want now.

I want a partner for life.

I want to be married again.

I'm looking for a man to age WITH me, at about the same pace, and have an agreed-upon vision for us.

So Many Others ...

CLEARLY, YOU GET THE picture that I've legitimately put myself out there and given several men a chance, but I just have not had any luck yet in finding a man who is emotionally available, stable, kind, and wanting an exclusive, committed relationship ... much less feeling that "spark."

I'll briefly bullet point the rest, just for kicks ...

- Met a kind, intelligent young man at "The Minimalists" seminar when they came to Chicago on a Wednesday night in April 2022.

  Although he lives in Michigan, we were still keeping in touch over several months over the "Telegram" app, because we exchanged phone numbers.

  We discuss "The Minimalists" book that we purchased at that seminar and both read, and other books we'd read, either in hard copy or on Audible.

  He wanted to come out from Michigan to see me on a weekend in downtown Chicago to hang out, but the connection faded, because I just wasn't attracted. We exchanged more pictures and such, but I wasn't "feeling it." So intelligent and kind, though!!

  Plus, he was another young one – like, in his early 30's. It's just not realistic. He'd want children someday, and

I have no interest in bearing more children, although I'd definitely be open to stepchildren in a heartbeat, because I love kids!

- Socially, I met another young gentleman who was kind and wanted to take me out, but then I learned he was involved with a married woman for quite a while who had an "open relationship" with her husband, and so I let that go. Besides, he has a drinking problem and anger issues. In fact, I would not doubt if he was on other drugs.

- Online, I met this very handsome 28-year-old father of four, but all he wanted to do was try and get me to "sext" with him, and I wasn't going to do that.

- Online, I connected with this guy who lived about 30 minutes away from me in a Southern town I kept bumping into on multiple dating sites, so I finally connected, and we chatted. He kept chatting, but never asking me out. Finally, he did, and when the day came, said he had got the address mixed up and it was further than he thought and if we could reschedule, but he never did. Blown off again, so I blocked him.

- Online, there was this guy from a Facebook singles party group who literally only sent me jokes or funny videos about once a week, but never asked me out.

- Online, I connected with this guy who literally looked just like Bret Micheals – long, blonde hair and all. He was from another country and had a cute accent.

We videochatted and it was a great conversation, but days went by, and he never asked me out and I don't like it when it gets into the "pen-pal zone," so I unmatched us.

- Online, I met this guy who was about 30 minutes from me in a Western suburb, but when we videochatted online, he must have been close to a decade older than all his pictures! I was very disappointed, and gently asked if his profile was up-to-date, and he said no, that I was the first one who "matched" with him in quite a while, because he's never on the site. It wasn't only that he looked older, but his energy was much slower than mine when we spoke, so I knew that wasn't going to work. Neither one of us messaged each other after that, so I unmatched us and made a note to always ask if their profiles were current from then on out.

- Became Facebook friends with a guy in a local band, but in conversation, discovered he's emotionally unavailable, because he's tied to a "Situationship." But that's okay, because he's also about 20 years my junior, so realistically, it's not what I'm looking for.

- Became Facebook friends with another local musician in a band who took a strong interest in me, who I was hopeful about, because he's tall (over 6'), handsome, and about my age ... only to discover he's living with his fiancé ... even though he's disclosed that he has

NO intention of marrying her any time soon, if ever. Disgusting! Poor lady!

- One of my Facebook friends I went to high school with confessed he had an interest in me, and we chatted a few times, but when push came to shove to meet up, he never did. Said he was working all the time and just stopped messaging.

- Coincidentally, I met the aforementioned guy's friend on Facebook dating. We also went to the same high school, but he was 3 years older than me. We chatted a few times, but then he got mad at me because I didn't remember something he told me and sent me this message below, and that was that.

> I have some Sat nights off.
>
> And it's that bar I told you about.
>
> You don't really remember a lot about what we talked about, if its cuz your dating other guys, then good luck. Not really into dating competitions. Good luck.

- Another guy I see socially, and is crazy about me, asked me out on a date. I accepted, but he never nailed it down. Unfortunately, he's got personal issues of his own. He's a sweetheart but needs help.

- Met another musician locally who had taken an interest in me, gave me his card, we exchanged numbers, and he seemed really kind and certainly talented. However, when I checked out his Facebook page, it was filled with a ton of crazy, negative stuff, and I was totally turned off.

  He texted me about a week later and I let him know what I found, and he just got all upset, defending it, saying he was "fighting for a cause."

  I wasn't on board.

  When I see him socially, I just pretend I don't. It's too awkward.

- Another gentleman I was Facebook friends with took a liking to me and asked me out to lunch. I went and it was nice. He's never disclosed he has any attraction to me, and I'm not one to make the first move anymore, so we never go "there" in conversation. However, I noticed whenever we chat, it's always about him being the "victim" in some situation that's happening to him, always some kind of drama.

  I don't like that.

  So, hopefully, he never says he's got an interest in me as any more than friends, so I don't have to hurt his feelings, but if he does, I'll be sure to be clear on mine, so I don't mislead him in any way.

- Online, met a local guy and we went on three dates. We were both divorced parents. He was thrilled that we had the same parenting schedule weekends, which is truly a bonus. However, he wanted to be exclusive after the 3rd date, and I was nowhere near ready for that, because this was early on when I was first stepping out, even pre-pandemic, so I said no. I wasn't all that attracted to him, anyway, although he was kind, so I let him go.

- I seem to get hit on all the time by men who are unhappily married. I make it very clear I don't mess with married men – these are a handful, so I'm just putting them all as one bullet here as a mention.

- Also early on, when I first got onto OK Cupid pre-pandemic, I met an extremely handsome young man in his 20's. We exchanged numbers and when I spoke to him on the phone, he sounded like he was completely wasted or else had a condition of some kind. He lived with his parents.

I tried to fish around to figure it out, but I never could. I told him I didn't feel we were a match and let him go.

But I kept bumping into him on other sites – Bumble and Facebook Dating. I said what the heck and matched with him again and we talked some more, but then I found out he lived way too far and didn't drive, so it just wasn't going to work out, and I finally let him go for good.

- The worst is when you see someone online who you know "IRL" (In Real Life) but aren't attracted to. A few times, I paid for a month subscription to Bumble to see my "beeline," which is that you get to see the men you "liked" you first. If you "like" them back, it's a match. I saw a guy I knew socially, but I just didn't like him in that way, so I never matched us.

  Once, we started chatting and he asked if I had seen him. I said I did, but that I wasn't on the dating sites anymore. I really didn't know what to say. He never asked about it since, thank God, because it turned out my friend was interested in him, so that took the focus off me, hopefully. I hate telling guys I'm not interested, but I am getting better at it, the more practice I get. It's the right thing to do to be upfront with them right away.

- Online (Facebook Dating), I met what seemed to be a really nice guy, but he got very creepy right away. I made the mistake of giving him my phone number, because I was able to look up his profile and he looked like a real person right in the next town over.

  Well, he changed the "theme" of our Messenger chat to "Love," which, I didn't even know could be done, and then he started saying how he was checking out all my photos and asked me if I believed in love at first sight and getting very serious very quickly.

  I did more digging, and it seemed to me like this poor guy's Facebook account was hacked by a scammer and the scammer was who I was talking to, not the actual guy, so I blocked him.

- I met a gentleman socially a few months ago who seemed kind and gentle, and so we exchanged numbers, which I thought was just friends. When he started texting me, it started off innocently, because he suggested things like going for a walk, getting ice cream, and accompanying him at the gym.

Then he started getting very complimentary about my body and saying I look like I'm in my 20's (I told him my age), and I thanked him, but let it go. It was when he sent me this that I cut it off:

> You have the cutest butt!
> So perky and firm makes me smile.

> If I could touch it it would feel like a soft cloud in heaven. Nothing wrong with touching.

> Can I touch your butt?

I told him to please stop, or I would have no choice but to block his number. He stopped and apologized, but I chose to block him anyway, because I was so creeped out.

Now when I see him socially, I pretend not to. It just shocks me that some men honestly think they could talk to women this way and that this is really going to work!

- Another one who cracks me up is another guy I see socially who literally licks his lips, smiles, and "sashays" over to me EVERY time he sees me, as if I'm some huge steak dinner. It totally creeps me out to the point of being disrespectful. It blows my mind what men think is sexy and going to attract a woman.

- Here was actually a very nice young man who was straight with me when I told him I was looking for a life partner. This was very refreshing:

> I may be a bit young for you to fill that need hun

> I understand! Thank you for being straight with me.
>
> Good luck on your search and take care!
>
> Have a great weekend!

- And I'll leave you with this winner – a response when I told this guy I'm getting off Facebook Dating:

Thank you as well gorgeous

Even if we never cross paths, I hope you have absolutely the best sex life possible! For a woman as stunning as you, absolutely. I mean that strictly as a compliment.

Hello, wow, um, that's a 1st, LOL!

So, aside from the above, I decided I'm done with online dating for good because of the following problems:

- They stop talking. The conversation fizzles after "a coupla, two-tree dayz" ... I began to end it after 3 days, when before I used to give them a week.

- In conversation, I'm asking better questions and getting better at identifying red flags, so I end it right away – it doesn't get very far and I'm sick of wasting my time.

- When I videochat with them, I discover they are not true to their profile in pictures – either don't look like their pictures, or way older.

- In videochat or phone conversation, I discover we don't have an "energetic connection" – not compatible energy.

- I discover that they are not true profiles – they are scammers/hackers.

- They want to get off the app right away and think you're scamming THEM if you don't give them your number.

- The few times I gave out my number, I had a scammer find me on Facebook and friend request me right away – I never gave him my last name or anything – I'm not even under my real or maiden name on Facebook, so I don't know how he found me. Folks can get too much information on you with just your phone number. Never again.

I'm proud of how far I've come from when I first "got back out there" in 2019. I used to just try and do "lunch dates" to learn how to even talk to men again after being married 17 years. I'd accept any offer of a date, even if I wasn't attracted to them. Then, the pandemic got me proficient in miscellaneous "Zoom dating."

At the rate I'm going, odds are I'll meet a wonderful man someday, and now that I've done my work, I'm in a much better place to receive him than I was before.

I mean, now I only invest my energies in those who demonstrate that they value me, and I lose interest in those who don't.

I know now that I have the power to keep myself safe in intimate relationships whereas I was too scared before.

I have the skills now that I didn't before to create health and well-being in my relationships.

Thank you, God! Amen!

The Road Ahead

Second Chances

I'M AWARE IT MAY look like I'm being harsh in many of these instances where I don't give these guys a second chance for making "mistakes" in scheduling time with me.

So, I want you to know that I AM a firm believer in second chances in relationships …

… as you saw when I told him back in March 2022 before he started his current job that "Hopefully, we get a second chance someday. We deserve it."

And he replied, "We do."

In fact, I went back to my ex-husband for a second chance at our marriage after filing for divorce from him in 2014.

I moved out, got my own place, lived there for about 7 months, and decided that I didn't want this life for my kids, so I went back to give my marriage a second chance.

About three months in, there was already trouble, but I fought hard for this with a solid action plan … I scheduled a family vacation, I had us rejoin our bowling league, I continued my own therapy, I found us a new (3rd!) marriage counselor, and I had my mom watch our kids while we went for those weekly marriage counseling sessions for a full year … before giving him the "ultimatum," which led to me filing for the second and final time.

So, despite my best efforts, my second chance didn't work for me. Rather, it ultimately confirmed that I had good reason to leave in the first place!

But I have NO regrets trying. I can look my children in the eyes and tell them that I did everything possible to save my marriage to their father and I am proud of that.

In fact, before I filed the first time, I took drastic steps to save it ...

... I stopped going out for my monthly "Gurls' Nights" with my high school friends that we started since our 30th reunion (because he didn't like that)

... I stopped making efforts to market my books (because he didn't like when I went on interviews and spent so much time on the computer)

... I took a month off Facebook (because he said I was on it too much)

... I went to my doctor and got a prescription for anxiety medication that I took for 6 months (because he said I thought I was "better" than him that I wasn't on medication for my anxiety and that I was "sitting there diagnosing him")

... I stopped exercising on Saturday mornings so that I could have breakfast with him and the kids (because he said my exercising instead of having breakfast with them was not helping us).

I fight for what is important to me.

That is why I'm big into talking things out to resolution.

Here is what Stephan Lebossiere has to say about it on Page 67 of his book "Finding Love After Heartbreak":

> "The door can always be opened to reconciliation and coming back together when the person is willing to come correct. Until then, it's not your duty to be a punching bag for anyone. Pray for people and keep it moving."

It's never the second chances that are the problem.

My mistakes are the third, fourth, and fifth chances I give.

Or should I say gave.

No longer.

But the trick also when you give that second chance is to make things perfectly clear.

Some people think just because they say something that the other person understands what they are saying.

The wise way to communicate is to always make sure that the other person has understood what you are trying to communicate.

If you don't care about whether or not the other person understands you, then you will never be in a successful relationship.

Guaranteed.

Wise men and women know how to communicate well.

If you find yourself in a series of unsuccessful short-term relationships (under five years, by my standards), then you really have to look at what it is you're doing wrong.

I know now what I have done wrong.

Now, it's just a matter of me finding that man who is also self-aware, and also willing to learn and grow as a person.

The sad part is that so many people don't.

They just don't care anymore about changing or growing as a person.

They have the attitude that "This is who I am and if they don't like it, they can leave."

Okay, that's great if you think you're perfect, like God!

But last I checked, no one is perfect. We all have room to grow and improve.

I believe that having a successful relationship also has to do with luck and blessings from God, for sure, but when you have that person in front of you, it is up to YOU to do the work to maintain it and nourish it just like a plant or anything else – like a business or your health.

ESPECIALLY if you are blessed enough to even GET a second chance!

You don't just work out one day and say, "Oh, I'm fine for the rest of my life now!"

No, it doesn't work that way.

You maintain your relationship every single day.

You do check-ins with your partner regularly.

You pay attention to your partner and do what you can to fulfill their needs as well as express your own needs and determine if your partner is also paying attention to you and doing what they can to fulfill your needs as well.

It's not 50/50, it's 100/100.

Like Mr. Miyagi said in "The Karate Kid," … "Do or do not. No in-between, or you get squashed like grape!"

Oddly enough, I was just about finished writing this book when I was told that the one I refer to as "he" is currently getting a second chance with his ex …

… and that it has been going on for over a year.

That would mean he reunited with her just about a couple of months or so after he ghosted me.

I admire that kind of resilience to be able to move on that fast! I sure wish I could be like that.

Apparently, it turns out his time with me was only a short break in his relationship with her.

He destroyed me emotionally, then picked back up right where he left off with her, "like a damn sociopath."

I got played.

Sadly, that also means this is yet another piece of important information the one I refer to as "she" has kept from me, which prevented me from healing much sooner.

She and I were still friends a year ago as of this writing (which is now September 2023). I didn't end the relationship with her until this March 2023.

I've been in this massive, debilitating pain for almost a year and a half.

A complete, broken mess.

I specifically asked her to let me know if he was seeing anyone to help me to move on.

Here was her reply:

> Honestly he hasn't even been around to do anything.
> He's been out of state.
> He has no time for women.

"Honestly," huh …???

She didn't tell me he was back with his ex when we started going out together again at the end of the summer after her surgery …

She didn't tell me in any of our texting in the fall …

She didn't tell me when I spent the morning with her on her team for her charity walk …

She didn't tell me when we were messaging over the holidays …

… and she didn't even tell me when we were having our heated text exchange over my birthday vacation.

Betrayer.

After everything I've done for her, she AGAIN repaid me with lies and kept relevant information from me …

… because she was loyal to him over me the entire time.

Had I known he was back with his ex, I could have moved on sooner, never consulted the psychics, and certainly never would have started messaging him again.

For over a year, I had been operating on her lie that "He's been out of state and has no time for women."

Perhaps if I had kept asking her if he had gone back to his ex, she probably would have told me.

Perhaps if I had asked who the "friend" was that he picked up his birthday cheesecake with at her place, she probably would have told me.

I want to believe that she kept things from me and lied to me in order not to hurt my feelings ... which obviously backfired and hurt me 10 times more in the end and also solidified my distrust in her.

On the other hand, she always did like his ex, so I'm sure she remained Facebook friends with her the entire time I was with him.

... and since she wanted us apart so badly, I wouldn't put it past her to have begun working with her to break us up in order to get THEM back together.

That would literally NOT surprise me at this point.

But seriously, it's probably best that I didn't discover this information any sooner, so that I could write this book.

I mean, up until just a few months ago, I was literally unable to sit down at the keyboard to even compile and write all of this ... because despite all my work, I was still in too much pain from the dual hit of both the ghosting AND losing a best friend.

Therefore, it was a blessing for me to discover that they are back together – and had been for over a year – because it was as they say "all I need to know" to finally let him go for good and move on.

I would NEVER try to break up a relationship by going after someone else's man.

That's just not who I am.

Plus, that would be bad Karma!

I disgraced myself by messaging him.

Although I can't help but wonder ...

Why couldn't he have simply replied to my first message and told me that he was back with her?

Why couldn't he have just said, "Stop messaging me."?

Instead of the "read-and-not-reply" torture for over an entire year, why didn't he just SAY any of the following words:

> "I'm done with you."
> "I don't want you in my life anymore."
> "I want nothing to do with you."

Better yet, why didn't he just block me from the start if he hated me this much?

Or ...

Why didn't he say the MOST important words ...

"I am back with *(my ex)*, and I love her."

Nevertheless, I hope he is finally happy with her now, because forgiveness and second chances are a good thing.

Fact = When BOTH people make the decision to do whatever it takes to make their relationship work, nothing can stand in their way.

I wish them luck!

I totally understand him trying again.

I believe it's good to really find out if she's the one or not, so that if it doesn't work out THIS time, he'll have no regrets.

This time if it ends again, he'll know for sure that he won't ever need to look back.

For me, I have that deep peace with my ex, precisely because I gave it that wholehearted second chance.

So, to me, giving that second chance was worth it, simply for that peace alone.

See, that's why I am so grateful that God is in charge, because it was truly Divine Timing for me to have discovered this information just as I was about done writing this book, anyways. It's a perfect ending for me.

It is exactly what I needed to know for me to be able to wrap this whole experience up neatly into this book and move on.

The Truth.

I have zero interest in men who are taken.

It's a total turn-off to me.

That is why I never date "separated" men, newly divorced, men or men who just ended a relationship.

And above all, I most certainly have NO interest in being someone's mistress for those married men who are too lazy, cheap, or broke to get divorced, but who choose to stay in loveless marriages, simply seeking a willing woman to consent to his situation so that he can have his cake and eat it, too.

No thanks.

And no engaged men, either!

My man is one who only has eyes for me, and I will not settle for anything less.

It's what every woman deserves.

Moving On

"Just move on!"

"Okay, it's been WAY too long … time to move on!"

"You really need to move on."

Yup.

I've been told this for the past year and a half and as you can see from the previous "My Healing Journey" chapter, I've done my very best.

This whole thing for me was perpetuated WAY too long because I gave my power away to the psychics.

Which, I'll NEVER do again.

(To be clear – it's not the psychics' fault, it's 100% mine.)

And it was also perpetuated by the fact that I really had deep feelings for him and felt a connection that – despite my best efforts to fight it – became out of my control.

And, whenever things are out of my control, I believe that it is in God's hands.

And, when he said that his schedule wouldn't be fair to me, I saw that as him having my best interests at heart.

And, thus, I took it as another clear demonstration that he really cared about me.

I mean, I believed we were going somewhere in our relationship, and that's the ONLY reason why I let him meet my kids on Mother's Day to give me that gift.

Then, the following week, he ghosted me.

It's unbelievable.

I thought that him getting this job and putting his life together would mean that when he was ready that the two of us could have a fresh start.

Apparently, that was a lie.

... or my imagination from his words.

He's merely resumed his relationship with his ex.

Apparently, I was under the wrong impression that he had any feelings for me at all.

I guess I was only hearing what I wanted to hear.

And that's just the way life goes.

All of that messed me up.

As many words as I've already written ... this entire book can't even fully explain the pain I've experienced.

... the devastation, confusion, despair, and humiliation.

... and the final knife in the heart finding out over an entire year later I've been in this pain that he ran right back to his ex, like I was nothing.

I was kept in the dark this whole time – just like they both kept me in the dark the last half of our relationship.

And that's why I hope and pray to help someone someday by sharing this experience, these lessons, so that no one else has to ever go through this – especially my kids someday when they are old enough to read this.

Ultimately, he forgot who he was and didn't act his best. He needed to be the King that (I'd like to believe deep down inside) he is, but instead, he lost himself in his insecurities and past relationship trauma.

I see now that the man I thought he was is not who he really is.

He showed me his true self by his choices.

I understand now that it was just my imagination and putting him on an unrealistic pedestal in my little fantasy world.

Looking at the big picture here, I see that he was NOT that great.

I see now he clearly just led me on and wasn't serious … unless perhaps he was once, then changed his mind.

I am also well aware that at this point, being at this job over a year and a half now, that he's most likely gotten on his feet financially, done all the things he wanted to do, and is now fully capable of getting a job locally to have a more stable schedule and reach out to me for that second chance we agreed that we deserved – but is choosing not to.

I accept that.

He was "familiar" to me, because he reminded me of the men in my family.

… except the men in my family don't abandon women, like this one does.

They are solid and reliable, unlike him.

He failed me.

He's broken my trust and image of him as a person.

I don't want a man like that in my life.

He did me a favor.

I don't have time for people in my life to be so easily persuaded to go against me and not treat me like a human being with the dignity of a simple response, if not a discussion.

Nonetheless, the experience served its purpose – another important lesson for me.

This is why I had to write this book = to sort this whole ordeal out and pass along what I've learned to those of us "on the path" who think like me.

It's now October 2023, as I'm still working on getting this book published.

It's been a month since I discovered the news that he's been back with his ex for at least over a year (if not more – I'll never know), which was right after he ghosted me.

I've been processing that.

... and still processing how my "best friend" at the time never told me.

... still processing how he never said a word all the times I was messaging him.

... been trying to cope with all that re-opened wound now.

... trying to understand how people can do this to others.

But, really, I'm not ALL that surprised, since I knew he was still communicating with his ex the entire time he was in a relationship with me.

He was upfront with me about that in the beginning, because he told me had a couple of financial ties to her that he "claimed" he could not get out of at the moment.

At the time, I felt that I had no reason not to believe him.

In my next relationship, I'll know better to steer clear of men who don't have an independent financial situation, and who are still tied to their exes – emotionally and/or financially.

I was very (too!) understanding with his ties to his ex.

That mistake was on me – I was trying to be understanding and not controlling.

Never again – I know my boundaries now.

This is why I've been watching all the relationship videos I can to learn from the coaches I've listed here.

They're helping me figure out how to screen these men early on for red flags and how to use my voice to stick to my boundaries and standards of how I deserve to be treated and what I'm looking for.

I didn't know I was dealing with an emotionally immature man.

... one who plays "3 Strikes" games

… one who thinks it's normal to leave his girlfriend alone at a bar

… one who has no problem never replying or reacting to messages

… one who is incapable of having an adult conversation

… one who is incapable of answering questions …

He was in bad shape as he was.

He most likely would not have made me happy in the long run.

I very well may have gotten the best of him when I did.

Given his history, that summer may have been the best he could do, and he may not ever be that happy again.

I'll never know.

What I DO know for sure is that I don't want to be with a miserable person.

I wanted him when he wanted to be better – the best version of himself.

Seems like he's given that up, so I definitely don't want that.

He did me a favor.

No one can predict the future – we create it for ourselves.

His second chance may or may not work out, although I hope for the best for everyone involved, since I know firsthand what it feels like to be devastated ... and so, I absolutely do NOT wish this feeling on anyone.

At least now, I'm more secure in who I am, and I have learned important lessons and relationship skills to better protect my heart (and my kids) going forward.

Thankfully, the publication of this book is going to be a huge catalyst in my "moving on" process ... finally.

I still do firmly believe that it is a blessing to know the truth – and still believe that it was the perfect time.

I realized last month that this was exactly what I needed to know to move on, let go, and allow the right man to come into my life ... finally.

Part of coping and healing for me is prayer and talking to God.

A huge thing I realized is that still ... my mind is being mean to me ... my thoughts are horrendous.

Because I don't know the truth of their relationship – only what I'm told via social media – my imagination is going haywire.

It's horrible.

One of my Prayer Chaplains turned me on to a Bob Newhart video on YouTube called "Stop It!". I highly recommend it – and watch the full 6-1/2-minute version – all the way to the end. It's utterly hilarious!!!

And, it truly has helped. I'm blessed to have such Angels in my life such as my Prayer Ministers to help me like this.

I think back to my relationship with him and all the things that were signs from God/The Universe that stopped us:

1. Her involvement ruining our relationship from "Date One" ... and throughout it all ... right up until his ghosting after his conversation with her.

2. His abandoning me that night and my breaking up with him the next day (if he didn't already consider his abandonment the breakup, which sounded like he didn't when he said "I wasn't even mad the next day").

3. Him losing his job, further ruining his already weak financial situation.

4. His getting sick over Halloween weekend ruining our plans (if that was even true).

5. My getting exposed to COVID and ruining our Christmas Eve plans.

6. Our New Year's Eve plans being ruined because the test at the pop-up mall shop wasn't conclusive (the guy literally said it looked like it was "a little bit positive") and then my Walgreen's results were damaged, and then I didn't get my negative test results on time.

7. I didn't win the vacation tickets (there was a radio contest), so I had to purchase both our tickets (which, he NEVER paid me back a DIME for his, by the way).

8. His passport package didn't come in on time, ruining our vacation, because now he couldn't go on the trip with me.

9. He chose to get a job that has him traveling for months at a time, indefinitely, ruining any chance of us getting back together, because that much time apart is definitely NOT the relationship I want to have with my man.

10. He chose to listen to her and cut me out of his life indefinitely, ending our relationship for good.

11. The gift he got me got run over by a car.

Obviously, God was telling me this man is clearly NOT meant to be with me.

When I think of it this way, that God did me a favor and was helping to protect me, that gives me more comfort.

Another friend told me to think of it this way = what if my NOT telling him my feelings WAS the right thing to do after all?

What if I should be congratulating myself for following my intuition that I knew he wasn't right, and it wasn't the right time to tell him how I felt about him, because he simply was NOT "my person" ... even though I thought he was?

... that it was NOT fear after all, but it was my intuition on point instead!!

Now, THAT thought/epiphany really does comfort me and help me to move on!

Instead of looking for all the social connections we have – making it likely that we would have met eventually – and all the other aspects that attracted me to him which I described in the previous chapter ... it's better for me instead to remind myself of the reality of all of this I listed above ... all the signs from God/The Universe, and ultimately, my own intuition upfront.

On top of all that, in hindsight, he and I had NO chance of a fair relationship with her and her situation, anyway ... it was one drama after another, aside from her sabotaging us.

I mean, first it was her first serious health issue, and we were both there for her for that ...

... then she was on our first date (and making fun of me)

... then she moved, and we were both there for her for that

...then she was sabotaging me behind my back

... then she had a death in the family, and we were both there for her for that

... then she had her second serious health issue, and we were both there for her for that

... it was all too much.

The odds were stacked against us.

We both had a type of "caregiver fatigue" with her.

And he was a mess.

Now, he and his girlfriend don't have to deal with ANY of that – they have it good!

That's why I'm sure they will be just fine this time around because she doesn't hang around him and this girlfriend, like she did when I was with him.

They don't have her messing with their relationship.

She didn't give him and I that kind of respect for our relationship.

He was too blind to see it.

Or maybe he just didn't care.

Maybe I was the blind one.

I hope his girlfriend at least knows that he and she slept together, so she's not being kept in the dark, like I was.

I needed that security and information on the front end, instead of having to keep figuring out what the truth was that whole time, since she was a person who kept things from me that I only found out after the fact.

What a significance honesty and transparency make in a relationship!

Regardless, my guess is if she were hanging out with them as much as she was with us, she'd cause problems between them as well.

Or, maybe his girlfriend would be more assertive than I and step up and open her mouth to say something, because she's not as close to her as I was.

Or maybe HE would actually step up and say something, because he loves his girlfriend and prioritizes her, since they actually had a committed relationship together and history – we didn't have any of that.

And now he's got a steady job.

Plus, someone said that she works at a dental insurance company, so he could marry her, get on her insurance, and finally get his teeth fixed, LOL! *(Hey. I gotta find some kind of humor in this to make myself feel better, right?)*

See ... it all worked out for the best for all concerned!

Realizing all this is very helpful for me to move on.

I knew something just wasn't right about him.

... despite how well he presented himself ...

... despite him doing all the right things in the beginning ...

... somewhere deep down, I knew.

So, I may have actually done the right thing after all!

Because I knew he wasn't in a good place.

And truth be told, neither was I.

I had financial problems at the time and with my issues I didn't even realize I had!

However at least I feel during all this time since then, I've cleaned up all of that (including my debt!) to the best of my ability at this point.

Back then, it just wasn't the right time for me, or for us.

Perhaps he was just a catalyst for me to learn all these lessons that I needed in order to prepare myself for the right man that God has for me.

I love the movie "Free Guy" starring Ryan Reynolds! Part of the storyline is that Ryan Reynolds was a "Non-Playing Character" in a video game who fell in love with a real character and needed to obtain certain achievements in the game to "level up" to be a match for her.

This was exactly the problem with him and I.

He didn't have certain life achievements to match with me.

- ✓ Stable job I am happy with
- ✓ Home I am happy with
- ✓ Reliable vehicle
- ✓ Finances in order
- ✓ No debt
- ✓ Good credit
- ✓ Work/life balance (to be able to enjoy life)
- ✓ Stable work schedule (to be able to plan events)
- ✓ Passport (to travel to all-inclusive resorts I enjoy!)
- ✓ Healthy smile

I mean, these are basic "adulting" things he didn't have.

She can have him, LOL!

I mean, seriously … not having all that was a problem – regardless of how I felt about him.

My feelings weren't enough.

IF he ever had feelings for me (I don't know because we never talked about it), it also wouldn't've been enough.

Therefore, he simply wasn't the right person for me.

Can people change?

Sure ... but it's unlikely.

Does it happen?

Yes.

Will it?

I don't know, and I can't dwell on that.

It's time to truly 100% focus on myself now as 2023 comes to a close these next few months and literally put this chapter in my life story to rest.

It's time to accept the reality of what happened – and why – and be at peace with it.

This is what moving on looks like.

I am secure now that all my warning signs and red flags about him were true.

The things that caused me not to have a relationship with him were valid.

He was my "transition person."

He showed me what I really want in a relationship and how I want to feel with a man.

I can once again trust my intuition.

And as far as "she" is concerned, I've seen her in public with another mutual friend, and we nodded hi to each other, which was nice. I will always be cordial to her in public like that because I have class. But, unfortunately, as of this writing, my kids and family don't know that she and I are no longer in each other's lives.

When my Mom asks about her, I just tell her that our schedules aren't lining up and/or she's very busy and/or she's just taking it easy because of her health issues and that she's doing just fine, because she is, as far as I know, which is a wonderful thing, because we all deserve peace in this world.

I will now do what my long-time counselor told me just before she retired, and that is "manage my ability to tolerate uncertainty in life."

I do not know what my future holds, and I'm okay with that, because now ...

I'm confident that I know what to do when it happens – or at least where to look for help, guidance, advice, and encouragement.

I'm so incredibly grateful for the people in my life who DO love me, care for me, respect me, and have my best interests at heart.

If I stumble and fall again, I know I will be picked back up.

And, through forgiveness and letting go ... with all the support I've received and will continue to receive ... with God's help ... with my own strength and resiliency ...

I know I will be okay.

Thank you, God!

Amen.

Self-Love

IF I LOVED MYSELF more, I never would have allowed them to treat me that way.

Having boundaries and standards for yourself is self-love.

That extends to how you take care of yourself, perform in your work, and how you treat others.

I try my best to treat others how I would like to be treated, and if it is brought to my attention that I made a mistake, I immediately apologize wholeheartedly.

That is also a form of self-love – maintaining my integrity and good character.

Because of my pain during this time, I wasn't functioning at my best and I feel everyone in my life was cheated.

When the ghosting first happened, I was probably at 50%.

When my gift broke probably 30%.

When I saw his message to our mutual friend confirming her involvement, probably 70%.

When she posted about his cake, I probably went back down to 50%.

I pulled myself back up over the following few months after the cake incident to probably about 90% at best.

Then, after I discovered they'd been together this whole time last month, I'm probably back down to 80%.

After this book is published and out into the world, I'll be finally able to let it go, and thus, I've made a plan for myself.

This plan includes actions to move on by doing extensive energy healing work, focusing on bringing my shattered Soul back ... regaining all my energy, so that I can function at 100% again.

Fortunately, also during this healing process, I found more self-love by getting back to my art.

I finally scanned all my old art that was small enough to scan, or else took pictures of the larger drawings and paintings, so that I now have a "digital portfolio," in case of damage to the originals.

I encourage everyone to get back to something that they love if you're not already doing it.

I believe everyone has an artist inside of them.

I consider art not only sketching, painting, and sculpting, but also:

- Writing
- Singing
- Playing an instrument
- Telling stories
- Telling jokes

- Being a tattoo artist
- Being a makeup artist
- Building things like houses
- Construction work
- Refurnishing homes
- Creating a garden of some kind (flora, fauna, or food)
- Decorating and maintaining your home

So much more!

Everybody is creative in some way.

Find that way and embrace it!

Use it to connect to your heart.

Aside from getting back to my art, my son has given me ukelele lessons, and a friend gifted me an acoustic guitar in which I plan to take lessons next year. I have two songs I've been wanting to learn for many years now – just those two, LOL!

I've also been practicing self-love by maintaining my exercise routine, although I have gained weight during this grieving time, now that this is finally over, I'm working on getting back to a weight that makes me feel better and less stressed. The number on the scale is not an issue – I know I still look good – it's just that because I'm short, I get winded more when I have this weight on me, that's all.

Also, I'm demonstrating self-love by being open and giving all these guys who approach me a chance – I'm not closing my heart, just because this one guy rejected me.

I definitely believe I deserve love and deserve to be treated with respect, kindness, and proper attention, and having my needs met in a relationship – as I would do the same for my man.

Unfortunately, I find that my loving, open heart attracts some very dark people.

So, at the time of this writing, I'm still not sure if I'm healed enough for a relationship.

But one thing I know for sure is that when I feel that way again about a man, I will recognize it, and I will know exactly what to do.

Because now, I have the resources and self-love to honor my boundaries and standards – and the resources to review when needed.

It's just going to be up to God.

I'm going to end this chapter with a beautiful true story to share.

A dear friend of mine dated this wonderful man about four years ago for a year and a half, but unfortunately, she had to let him go, due to life circumstances.

They both dated other people. She had a 10-month relationship, and he had about a 3-year one.

Earlier this year, by the Grace of God, he came back to her.

He had done extensive self-work, and so had she.

They both have that "we" mindset and are taking their time.

Although they consider themselves "officially" dating for only a few months as of this writing, they have been "talking" for about half a year now.

They are both madly in love and I couldn't be happier for her – for them both! He's a great guy and I see they truly are perfect for each other.

She tells me when it's the right person, you'll know – the circumstances will be right, he'll make the effort, you'll be able to talk and laugh about everything, and he'll bring you joy.

Exactly everything all the videos say.

Best part ... she is 53 so at least I could still have 3 more years to go before I find mine – I have hope!

My One

FIRST AND FOREMOST, MY man will have done the work on himself as I have. This means, he's done his best to understand his own issues, heal his own emotional triggers, and learn to regulate his own emotions, as I have done my best to do.

Secondly, has he done the work on himself to clear any bad thoughts, bad energy, and ties with his ex – both emotional and financial.

Thirdly, he is interested in being "a partner." I am clear that I want to be a wife again. He would be interested in being a husband to me ... willing to work on us for the rest of our days.

These three things are about equally important, so that we are both 100% present and ready to "give it our all" in this relationship.

If those things are established with him, then my ideal relationship with him is one that is mutually fulfilling, exclusive, and committed.

Therefore, he must be a man who CAN commit.

He'll have the wisdom, temperament, patience, and love for me to handle my anxiety and "Anxious Attachment" style, as I would do for him in whatever his issues are.

Our relationship would be one that is fun, passionate, vibrant, emotionally healthy, and thriving because we both pour into each other's needs, while working towards being the best version of ourselves, and overcoming any obstacle together.

One where there's trust, loyalty, and respect, continuing to learn and grow together in our partnership and committing to upholding each other's highest and best good, even when it's challenging.

One where we are emotionally attuned, emotionally connected, emotionally stable, and mutually respectful.

One where I am heard, seen, and appreciated fully, never feeling judged, rejected, or shamed.

One with a man who wants to share his LIFE with me – not "one night," or "a few months to a year." *(As of the answer options in OK Cupid to the question "How long do you want your next relationship to last?)*

One who understands that we'll have conflicts and difficulties, but that our relationship and having each other in our lives is worth working through them, because we value each other that much.

I'm looking for a man who, like me, understands that we are always a work in progress.

He'll have the resolve to handle whatever issues arise and is interested in deepening our connection time and time again.

One who doesn't have an addiction ... not to alcohol, drugs, his phone, or his job.

In fact, when we're out and if I'm losing track of time, he'll let me know when it's time to leave ... because he'll prefer to leave at a reasonable time with me, instead of closing out a bar.

He won't be a "complainer" or ruin dates with his negativity.

I mean, I'm 50 now, I don't have time to waste being miserable. I want to focus on the joy and good in life that we can. The rest of the world is a mess right now as it is, so we can create our own peace in our own home and relationship together – our own little haven.

We'll have a home together.

I want a patio with "Fairy Lights." I think those are so incredibly beautiful!

And, if not fairy lights, then "Tiki Torches" again.

By a lake again ... or, better yet, a river or pond – any kind of water.

I want a basement again.

I want my pool table again.

And my dart board.

I want a home again big enough to entertain all our friends and family, like I used to.

I want him to have a good sense of humor! I want to be able to laugh with him every day. We can send each other funny memes or watch comedy shows together.

Someone to shoulder the burdens and to share the joys of life with.

A man who would be willing to build a beautiful, healthy, thriving, purpose-filled relationship with me.

He would WANT to listen to what I have to say and value my feelings.

He would ask me questions about myself to want to know me.

A man who is willing to talk through issues is the one for me, because that shows me that he values me in his life.

He would be my "Safe Space."

Someone I can trust and count on.

A man I can be comfortable with.

A man I can be myself with.

I can talk to him and feel he is listening and that my feelings and opinions matter.

We can talk about topics for hours that matter to us.

A man who will work at a happy fulfilling relationship.

Our dialogue on bringing up issues or red flags would be focused on growing and deepening our relationship, not breaking it down.

We could tell each other every day at least one thing we are grateful for about each other and do regular check-ins.

An emotionally mature and healed man, at least enough to keep working at it – perhaps we heal our issues together as we navigate the relationship and ride the storms.

A man who considers me Gold.

… and he would never let me doubt it.

He would make me feel I'm the most beautiful woman in the world and best lover he's ever had – even if it isn't true – he'd make me feel that way.

He'd make me feel that he only has eyes for me and would not pay attention to other beautiful women in my presence – and without my presence – because he loves me.

A man who considers me / our relationship a priority in his life, besides his kids, because he values me and the life we are creating together.

A man who is willing to do what it takes to make our relationship work, such as being honest, talking things out to resolution (instead of just walking away), and being interested in his woman's happiness as much as his own.

We both do things to support our mutual respect and harmony to increase warmth and intimacy between us.

One who knows what it takes to be in a relationship – that it's not all about himself. He'll have "we" mentality.

He will have the maturity to listen, the respect to understand, and the commitment to find a solution.

Ultimately, I desire a strong man who can make me feel safe to be his woman.

My Ideal Man could bring me security and I could bring him peace.

He wants to enjoy life and experiences.

A man who I can fall asleep with and wake up next to every day.

Or, if this ideal man travels for his job, then I figured out that my threshold is probably not more than 2 weeks without him by my side – not much longer than that. *(This is because I currently have my kids every other weekend, so it would work out perfectly fine for me – on my kid days, I'm too busy to miss him too much!)*

If push came to shove, I could maybe sustain something longer than that for about 6 months, if we were in a committed, exclusive relationship, but beyond that, it would be too painful for me to deal with, and I don't believe that much time apart would be beneficial for our relationship at all – I may as well remain alone in that case.

For me, if he's never around, then what's the point.

Not that I would have to cheat, I'm just saying that it would be unfulfilling – that much time apart on an indefinite basis is definitely NOT what I want, ultimately.

I want someone to go home to at the end of the day who actually cares how my day went.

A man to be with me on a regular, permanent basis – to be a part of my day-to-day life – to do all the activities we enjoyed together – to travel and plan things with …

… and especially being on some kind of weekly team together. I loved that and I really want that again! Preferably volleyball, bowling, or pool – something we both enjoy together and keeps us fit and active.

At the end of the day, I want what Jonathan Asley outlines here as "Real Love" … I need my man's attitude to be:

> I'm here
> You matter
> WE are important
> I've got your back
> I'm not going anywhere
> I only want YOU
>
> Someone who WANTS to be "a partner"

That's always been my attitude.

Just can't seem to find that in a man …

… yet.

Although there are many wonderful men out there, "there can be only one" for me.

Current Strategy

So, MY CURRENT STRATEGY in finding my "One" is ...

NOTHING.

No more positioning anyone as my "mediator," and certainly no more psychic readings, vision boards, soul cards, "visioning," Claddagh rings, rose quartz pendants, affirmations, dating sites, singles groups ... nothing.

I mean it.

No more praying for strength – I have it.

No more praying for peace – I found it.

No more praying for "my person" to find me – I no longer "need" him to.

If that day comes, however, I now understand that I won't even know if he's "my person" until about 3-6 months in.

So, in the meantime, I'm still working on me – being the best "me" that I can be – the best Mom, Friend, Business Colleague, Creative, Teacher, Volleyball Player, Bowler, Pool Player, Singer that I can be!

This way, I will continue to have SO much to offer that lucky man!

... the man that I expect great things from in return, if he happens to show up in this lifetime.

Rest assured, for the rest of my days here, I'll remain happily "grooving along" in my life, regardless.

What I've learned is that love makes no sense.

You can't plan it.

You can't force it.

You can't fake it.

It doesn't matter how long people have been together.

It happens out of the blue and changes your life forever.

It's truly a gift from God.

It doesn't have to be showcased or posted about.

It doesn't have to be explained to anyone.

Love just is.

There's no controlling it.

There's not even any tangible "proof," honestly.

You can't look at a picture of a couple and "see" if they love each other or not.

It's just a feeling.

You just know.

That's exactly why I'm no longer praying for it ...

I'm only praying to be ready when it finds me again.

Letting Go

THIS YEAR'S LENTEN BOOKLET at my church held particularly significant meaning for me (2023). It was titled "40 Days of Letting Go" by Unity World Headquarters, www.unity.org.

Every day there was a passage about letting go of something, such as anxiety, anger, blame, etc.

The introductory story was called "Easter is Our Story," and it talks about how Jesus' crucifixion, entombment, and resurrection is in parallel to the story of our lives in that we also metaphorically cycle through those processes repeatedly in one way or another – these metaphorical deaths we experience.

It also reminds us there is always a dawn. Always a resurrection. The sun always rises again.

Regardless of how much pain we have gone through or are currently in, having the faith to "let go and let God" is how we find the strength and the will to be victorious in doing so.

That's always been a challenge for me – not the part about having faith in God, but the part about letting things go.

I'm working on this.

Some issues are too important to me that I simply won't stop until I get answers – it's something I must do.

I drive people crazy who don't understand or don't have the patience for it.

Nothing is ever over until *I* say it is.

Not until *I* am satisfied and have my resolution.

I see now … how arrogant that attitude is!

That is my ego at its finest, alright!

How sad.

My old counselor said that perhaps something helpful for me to work on is "manage my ability to tolerate uncertainty in life."

She was 100% correct.

I don't like not knowing all the information and facts and what's going to happen in the future.

I like to be prepared, so that I'm not caught off-guard.

Not only do I have a "Plan B," but a "Plan C, D, and E."

I realized in all my self-work that I try to control anything and everything I possibly can in my life – all my time, my kids' time, whatever projects I put my mind to, my health and fitness, and the way I want things to work in life.

Yes, that means I am a tremendously accomplished person ... but in dating and relationships that mindset just doesn't work.

Sometimes, there is no resolution.

Some people will give you no answers.

To master acceptance of this and what to do with that has finally given me peace.

In the writing of this book and doing all the work I've done on myself – identifying and healing my own issues, analyzing everything that's happened and finding my own answers – I finally have my resolution.

NOW, it's over.

Those people who stuck by me along the way ... that's how I've come to find who is "for" me and who is not.

My determination and faith have been my saving grace – along with those people I listed in my dedication – that has gotten me through the pain.

I let go and know that I am not in charge – God is.

If I am meant to find my One in this lifetime, that's up to God.

If I am meant to live alone the rest of my days in this lifetime, that's up to God.

For so long, I had been SO angry, admonishing myself for knowing better, but now, I remember this – hindsight is always 20/20.

If I knew better, I'd have done better.

All I can do is my best.

I happen to believe that others are doing their best as well with their own experiences and lessons in life.

I give myself grace and I extend it to others.

I'm done beating myself up over trusting the wrong people, saying the wrong things, and making the wrong decisions.

I let go.

I would get SO angry at my dear friend every time she told me that.

I would tell her I AM! I AM "letting go!" Quit saying that! I'm TRYING! Can't you see that?

Well, no, she couldn't see that because I wasn't letting go.

This book is my letting go.

It needed to be written.

I needed to tell the truth of what happened.

And NOW, I can finally let it go.

I release all attachments and find peace in the life I have created for myself and my children.

I let go.

When the pain wants to creep back into my thoughts and feelings …

I let go.

If anyone wants to try and bring me down, I pray for their highest good.

I let go.

I may have to reread my Lenten booklet *(and the lessons in this book I've written right here!)* time and time again, to keep practicing, but ultimately …

I let go.

Dear Reader, do whatever it takes for you to find your peace.

Let them go.

Conclusion

THIS BOOK WAS WRITTEN to show you how insidious and cruel one person can be to a relationship ...

Yourself.

Fighting my own mind was the toughest battle I've ever fought in my life.

I took the time to be alone to figure myself out and connect with God.

Writing this book has been so cathartic for me.

It took me to so many places ...

I was even surprised at what popped out.

In fact, in the middle of writing this book, I reached the 5-year anniversary of my divorce.

Now, believe me when I say that I could write a whole other book about the State of Illinois legal system and what I had been through fighting for my children's wellbeing, but I won't for their sake.

In fact, I WAS going to write that book originally – about my entire divorce ordeal – but I was more inspired by the subject of dating and relationships, because not only did I have plenty to say about that, but in my opinion this subject seemed more all-encompassing, relevant, useful, and purposeful than the latter idea.

I feel like this book basically wrote itself – I finished 98% of it within about three weeks once I got started.

It's been the culmination of all the work I've done on myself to heal those parts of me I didn't realize were still unhealed until "The Ordeal" brought it out in me.

I have finally released all false hopes I had from listening to others by empowering myself instead.

I've been able to release all my painful memories and glean the lessons behind them.

Now, for me, "The Ordeal" is finally completely and truly over, and I can be at Peace.

I literally made an incredibly painful experience merely a chapter in my life – not the whole story.

I have created a collection of personal lessons as my own relationship guidebook to use for myself and to share with others.

I want all those listed in my "Dedication" to know that I'm alright now.

To those of you reading this who know my situation and exactly who I'm speaking about, please know that this book was my release to focus on the lessons learned – NOT the nitty gritty of the dirt that happened.

I have zero interest in dwelling in all that pain, nor disclosing the names of who these people are, because I need to finally move on. I only wish all of us peace.

Lessons learned for us all.

If anything, I hope this book teaches people to stop this ghosting BS, grow a spine, and have a tough conversation.

Or, at least an explanation.

Look what it can do to someone.

It's a horrible thing to do and bad Karma on you.

After all of this, another important thing I've learned is that being your own Guru means honoring yourself and your feelings.

Even if you are misunderstood, your feelings are what YOU are feeling and they should be honored, recognized, and validated by yourself.

You need to take care of your emotional and mental wellbeing first in order to be the best for everyone else ...

And not the other way around, as we so often do.

Just like "he" said he was doing when he recognized that he was "angry too often and that's not fair to others."

If anyone reading this is in a new relationship or struggling in a current one, I highly recommend watching my "Relationship Gurus'" videos on YouTube and other social media: Jay Shetty, Matthew Hussey, Stephan Lebossiere, Matthew Coast, and Jonathon Asley.

Follow Cody Bret to learn how women should be treated and to understand what a healthy, thriving relationship looks like. He clearly outlines a beautiful standard.

Subscribe to Trent Shelton's YouTube videos and podcasts for motivation and support. He's helped me tremendously over the years. I also get his daily texts.

I still consider myself a work-in-progress, but at least now I can safely say I know myself better than I did two years ago, and that I now have resources to fall back on if and when I need them in the future.

I will never stop working on improving myself.

After everything I've been through, I deserve a good life.

I deserve all the happiness I am experiencing now.

I am grateful that I am finally focused on myself and learned all these lessons, so as never to have that happen to me again.

I pray each and every one of you are happy and at peace – coupled or uncoupled.

God Bless and Namaste!

List of Lessons

1. Always do an internet search on who you plan to date.

2. You never know when or where God will have you meet someone special.

3. Don't feel compelled to inundate a new partner with the details of your previous relationship(s).

4. Some relationships come into your life for a reason, but not meant to last.

5. Only date someone emotionally available.

6. Trust your intuition.

7. There needs to be boundaries between friendships and romantic relationships.

8. When someone sets you up with somebody of the opposite sex that they claim is "a friend," make sure you find out the extent of their history first, and if you're comfortable with that, before you consider pursuing that relationship.

9. Be on the same page as your partner in sexual ethics and morals and if different, make sure to respect yourself; honor your boundaries.

10. Don't let anyone minimize your feelings. Do not dismiss your feelings or let anyone talk you out of them.

11. First instincts are often correct.

12. If in doubt about something you heard about your partner, ask them. Do not make assumptions.

13. Don't ever agree to a "casual" relationship with someone you have feelings for.

14. If you are blessed to have someone in your life you are happy being coupled with, let them know how you feel about them.

15. If the feelings are mutual, lock it down, and then proceed do what it takes to make it work, riding the natural challenges that will cross your path by working through them, because you feel being with that person is worth it.

16. Never allow a third party to interfere with your romantic relationship – A relationship is between two people.

17. Nobody has the authority to speak on behalf of anyone else, no matter how long they've known each other. So, if somebody tries to speak on behalf of your partner, discuss it directly with your partner as soon as possible.

18. Never be afraid to talk to your partner about issues involving third-party interference – it is important to give them a chance to see how they react – to find out if you are on the same page regarding the value of your relationship.

19. Speak up!

20. Learn your partner's preferred communication style and use it.

21. Keep written communication to a minimum.

22. Keep deep feelings for in-person conversations.

23. Your friends are not your counselors.

24. Jealousy stems from insecurity.

25. Do not unleash all your insecurities onto your partner – deal with it via a counselor, far-removed friends, a Prayer Ministry, journaling, praying, or any other avenue, so that you come to your partner clear-headed. Your insecurities are not their problem.

26. Jealousy has no place in a healthy relationship – romantic, friendship, business, or otherwise.

27. People can achieve emotional intimacy over time.

28. The number of years in a relationship is not what matters – it's the quality of the connection that matters.

29. If there is something you need from someone in a relationship – be it an apology or an explanation – make that request as soon as you can.

30. Do NOT ignore your needs. Do NOT sweep them under the rug to let it fester for months on end.

31. Never allow a conversation to proceed when it crosses the boundary of insults, name-calling, referencing third-party information, or a bad connection.

32. Don't block people out of anger in the moment. Make sure you table the conversation for another time to resolve things.

33. Make sure alcohol isn't ruining your relationships.

34. If your partner gets angry when you ask questions about them, that's a huge red flag.

35. Don't imprison yourself with the idea of "loyalty" or "obligation" where abuse, disregard, and lack of appreciation is happening.

36. Never introduce a partner to your school-age kids until you are in a committed, exclusive relationship.

37. Learn to recognize a toxic relationship and end it.

38. Learn to make requests.

39. There is a "right way" and a "wrong way" to apologize. Follow those bullet point characteristics listed in

the referenced article to ensure it is a sincere "True Apology."

40. Don't automatically count out a potential partner because you believe them to be "too different." Get to know someone on the inside – how they think, what their character is like, what their plans are, what motivates them.

41. A breakup or divorce is a valid reason to mourn and get help for grieving.

42. Do NOT give your decision-making power in your relationship over to anyone else. You are your own authority. YOU are your own "Guru."

43. Make decisions based on the facts you have on hand – not imaginary possibilities that you have no basis to believe.

44. Do NOT mess with Karma. Be cognizant of your actions and do your best to make amends with people to the best of your ability. If you need to end a relationship, send them off in peace and do NOT do or say things to purposely hurt them or wish them harm in any way.

45. Learn the warning signs of mental health conditions.

46. Let the fear of loss go; focus on and cherish the love that you feel, that you have right before you while you can, right now in the moment that you are given and

blessed with as the gift that it is, that's why it's called "the Present."

47. Trust yourself. Know your boundaries, wants, needs, and expectations; communicate them to your partner early on; make requests when a boundary is crossed or a need unmet; walk away when those requests are unfulfilled.

48. Forgiving our exes is a huge part of being healed and ready for a relationship. Make sure you've done your work before getting involved with someone. Don't think that a new relationship will solve your old wounds, because it won't – you'll just end up bleeding those old wounds onto the new person.

49. Do the work it takes to process through any unresolved pain and hurt lingering from your past.

50. Make lemonade out of lemons. Be grateful for what you have.

Memes to Remember

IF SOMEONE IS STUPID enough to walk away from you, be smart enough to let them go.

You can't start the next chapter of your life if you keep re-reading the last one.

If you never heal from what hurt you, you'll bleed on people who didn't cut you.

Dang, this man just said … Broken men know who to love but not how to love. Broken women know how to love, but not who to love.

You can't go back and change the beginning, but you can start where you are and change the ending.

I'm fixing me. Because sometimes I'm the Problem.

What you're attracted to when you're broken, disgusts you when you're healed.

What It Was: It was what it was to me. And that doesn't change no matter what it was (or wasn't) to you.

Sometimes it's better to just let things be, let people go, don't fight for closure, don't ask for explanations, don't chase answers and don't expect people to understand where you're coming from.

Don't let the heart that didn't love you keep you from the one that will.

Being single is smarter than being in the wrong relationship.

Standing up for yourself doesn't make you argumentative. Sharing your feelings doesn't make you oversensitive. And saying no doesn't make you uncaring or selfish. If someone won't respect your feelings, needs and boundaries, the problem isn't you; it's them.

People who can't communicate think everything is an argument.

Saw a quote that said … "Thank you for letting me go, because I wouldn't have walked away" and that hit different.

A conversation about how you feel is not supposed to end in an argument.

If I did something wrong, communicate. If I hurt your feelings, make me aware. If I didn't listen well enough, tell me again in a way I'll understand. If I'm insensitive to your needs, to your desires, or to your thoughts, tell me so I can consider them. But don't hold an attitude with me because you haven't clearly expressed yourself. I'm human, not a mind reader.

There is something uniquely beautiful about a person that grows from their struggles and uses the lessons from their experiences to spread wisdom. I don't care what you did or how far you fell. Be the example that shows others that they can overcome that mountain too.

Yes. Relationships take work. We have to work hard to not behave like a child when we're triggered. We have to work hard to heal our pasts. We have to work hard to be accountable when we want to blame. This is why if you want a relationship, you better be ready to open up, be brave, and break your patterns. Because even with the right person you'll have to face yourself.

I used to think that communication was key until I realized comprehension is. You can communicate all you want to someone but if they don't understand you, it won't reach them the way you need it to.

Strange, isn't it? You know yourself better than anyone else, yet you crumble at the words of someone who hasn't even lived a second of your life. Focus on your own voice, it's the only one that matters.

The awesome moment when these two finally decide to synchronize (brain and heart).

Sometimes what didn't work out for you really worked out for you. Read it again.

Respond, don't react. When things don't go as expected, pause and consider what's going on. You can control your emotional reactions to situations, but only if you respond consciously.

Impulstive reactions driven by extreme emotions like frustration and anger lead to s#!++y decisions and unnecessary suffering.

I really wanted it to be you, I so badly wanted it to be you, until I understood you didn't want it to be me.

Life goes on, with or without whoever and whatever. Never forget that.

Communication is good, but understanding is everything.

Don't be afraid to get back up again, to try again, to love again, to live again and to dream again. Don't let a hard lesson harden your heart.

Breathe, Sis. This is just a chapter. It's not your whole story.

I overthink because I overlove and I overcare.

Trust can't live in the same space as secrets and lies.

A lie is a lie. A white lie is a lie. A half-truth is a lie. A hidden truth is a lie. A lie by omission is a lie.

Never let someone make you believe that your gut instincts are just your insecurities playing tricks on you.

I read somewhere, "you keep forgiving someone until you unlove them," and I felt that.

I can respect any person who can put their ego aside and say, I made a mistake, I apologize, and I am correcting the behavior.

Forgive and forget is a myth. It's healthy to remember so you can create exquisite boundaries so the act isn't repeated.

I never knew how strong I was until I had to forgive someone who wasn't sorry, and accept an apology I never received.

Forgiveness has nothing whatsoever to do with how wrong someone else was; no matter how evil, cruel, narcissistic or unrepentant they are, when you forgive a person, you break the unhealthy bonds between you and your abuser-victim relationship, and you redefine yourself as an independent victor in your own life.

Forgiving someone may cost you your pride, but not forgiving them will cost you your freedom.

Forgiveness is not always easy. At times, it feels more painful than the wound we suffered, to forgive the one that inflicted it. And yet, there is no peace without forgiveness.

Forgiveness is not something we do for other people. We do it for ourselves – to get well and move on.

Forgiveness. Anyone can hold a grudge, but it takes a person with character to forgive. When you forgive, you release yourself from a painful burden. Forgiveness doesn't mean what happened was OK, and it doesn't mean that person should still be welcome in your life. It just means you have made peace with the pain, and are ready to let it go.

Making yourself happy again is the biggest comeback.

The way people view you.

Sometimes I think about the different characters I play in everybody's story.

I'm a terrible person in some people's narratives and a Godsend in others.

And none of it has anything to do with the person I truly am.

The lens that others view you through is colored by their upbringing, beliefs, and individual experiences.

Some people see your bright personality as endearing and others see it as annoying.

Some people think you're weak and emotional and others feel safe to be themselves around you.

Some people think you're rude and selfish and others respect the way you stand up for yourself.

Some people admire the way you take pride in the way you look, and others think you're conceited.

And none of it has to do with who you truly are as a person.

What you have to understand is that you have no authority over how people view you so never try to control the way others see you because the only thing that truly matters when the dust settles down at the end of the day is what you genuinely see in yourself.

~ Cody Bret

1 Corinthians 13:13 ~

"And now these three remain:

Faith, Hope and Love.

But the greatest of these is Love."

Printed in the United States
by Baker & Taylor Publisher Services